Lecture Notes in Business Information Processing 177

Series editors

Wil van der Aalst
Eindhoven Technical University, Eindhoven, The Netherlands
John Mylopoulos
University of Trento, Povo, Italy
Michael Rosemann
Queensland University of Technology, Brisbane, QLD, Australia
Michael J. Shaw
University of Illinois, Urbana-Champaign, IL, USA
Clemens Szyperski
Microsoft Research, Redmond, WA, USA

W0235101

For further volumes:
http://www.springer.com/series/7911

Joseph G. Davis · Haluk Demirkan
Hamid R. Motahari-Nezhad (Eds.)

Service Research and Innovation

Third Australian Symposium, ASSRI 2013
Sydney, NSW, Australia, November 27–29, 2013
Revised Selected Papers

 Springer

Editors
Joseph G. Davis
University of Sydney
Sydney, NSW
Australia

Hamid R. Motahari-Nezhad
IBM Almaden Research Center
San Jose, CA
USA

Haluk Demirkan
University of Washington
Tacoma, WA
USA

ISSN 1865-1348   ISSN 1865-1356 (electronic)
ISBN 978-3-319-07949-3   ISBN 978-3-319-07950-9   (eBook)
DOI 10.1007/978-3-319-07950-9
Springer Cham Heidelberg New York Dordrecht London

Library of Congress Control Number: 2014941700

Printed on acid-free paper

Springer is part of Springer Science+Business Media (www.springer.com)

Foreword

The Australasian region can be justifiably proud of its vibrant community of researchers and practitioners committed to services research and innovation. The Service Science Society of Australia represents this community and seeks to promote service innovation in all sectors of the Australian economy.

The society organizes the annual Australian Symposium on Services Research and Innovation (ASSRI), which also serves as its annual meeting. The first two symposia in this series were primarily community-building events. The Third Australian Symposium on Services Research and Innovation, which took place November 27–29, 2013, in Sydney, was a much larger event with many new features. Firstly, it put together a rigorously refereed research track with an international Program Committee. Secondly, it included three keynotes from international speakers: Eric Dubois (Public Research Centre Henri Tutor, Luxemburg), Christof Weinhardt (KSRI, Germany), and Jean-Jacques Dubray (Convergence Modelling LLC, USA). Thirdly, there were many industry-led invited presentations on service innovation topics in the areas of big data, e-health services, service compliance, and creative industries. Finally, there was a Panel Discussion around the Future of Service Science facilitated by Hamid Motahari (IBM Research Almaden).

These are the proceedings of the ASSRI 2013 research track, which represent the best in innovative thinking from this community (and beyond). These papers also reflect the progress toward achieving a multidisciplinary synthesis of approaches to address services research challenges.

April 2014   Fethi Rabhi
                                                                        Aditya Ghose

Preface

Service Research and Innovation: Emerging Developments

In recent years, there is a growing recognition among researchers and policy makers of the primacy of the service sector in the overall economic landscape of both developed and developing countries. This, however, is not fully reflected in the research priorities of universities, research agencies in both the public and private sector that engage in applied research, and funding bodies world-wide. The productivity levels in the service sector continue to lag behind the traditional goods-based manufacturing, mining, and agricultural sectors. Yet, service industries offer significant potential for large-scale innovation and productivity growth by exploiting the developments in information, communications, and related technologies. Moreover, the gap between goods and services-based industries is narrowing as a result of what has come be to be referred to as the "servitization" of many of the activities in the goods production life cycle.

The papers included in this edited book represent a small sample of contemporary research that attempts to document and advance the transformative role of the evolving service sector and to expand on the critical role of the information and communications technologies (ICT) in this transformation. The contributions are multidisciplinary in scope and cover strategic, organizational, and technological dimensions. They range from purely conceptual to concrete implementations and testing of service-related technological platforms. Taken together, these papers provide a snapshot of the critical concerns and developments in service-related research and cover some of the key areas of research focus.

The eight contributions included in this volume were selected from the 18 papers submitted to the Third Australasian Conference on Service Research and Innovation held in Sydney, Australia, during November 27–29, 2013. Each paper received three reviews. Based on the reviews, the authors of the selected papers were given the opportunity to revise and resubmit their papers for publication in this proceedings volume.

The first two papers by Vijaya Murthy and Olivera Marjanovic ("Understanding a Transformation Process from Product-Centric to Customer-Centric Services in a Financial Institution – A Work System Perspective") and Eng K. Chew ("An Integrative Design Framework for New Service Development") provide a coherent characterization of the "service system," which constitutes the basic unit of analysis in the broader discourse on services and service economy. The central thrust of the Murthy and Marjanovic paper is on the transition from a *product-centric* to a *customer-and-service-centric view of* organizations and the strategic, cultural, and organizational changes that this transition entails. The transition process is analyzed through the theoretical lens provided by work systems theory (WST). The empirical segment of the paper is a comprehensive case study of a financial services company that details the transition of its services structured around specific financial products to new ones re-designed around the customer. This paper illustrates the main challenges and tensions during three distinct phases of the transition and provides a glimpse of the competitive effects of the transformation. Eng K. Chew adopts a normative design perspective. He proposes and exemplifies a customer-centric, integrative design framework for new service development (NSD). The need for the design framework to be aligned with the organization's service strategy is emphasized.

The next three papers by Chhetri et al. ("Smart Cloud Broker – Test Drive the Cloud Before You Buy"), Karunakaran et al. ("Decisions, Models and Opportunities in Cloud Computing Economics: A Review of Research on Pricing and Markets"), and Joukhadar and Rabhi ("Effective Governance During SOA Lifecycle – Theory and Practice") deal with the technology infrastructure for services in general and service computing in particular. Cloud platforms and service-oriented architecture models in combination offer one of the most significant technological innovations that has transformed the way many services are conceptualized and delivered. The paper by Chetri et al. makes an important contribution to the problem of cloud vendor selection by developing and testing the Smart CloudBench, which is a suite of software tools that enables prospective purchasers of cloud infrastructure services to test drive the diverse offerings and to select the best alternative based on price, specification profile, and performance. This automated, on-demand, and customizable tool has been tested extensively and has the potential to take much of the guesswork out of cloud service acquisition decisions. Karunakaran et al. provide a comprehensive review of the key decisions and models in the context of the economics of cloud computing. Joukhadar and Rabhi highlight the importance of service-oriented architecture (SOA) governance and attempt to analyze the gap between theory and practice in this area. This paper also identifies the specific roles of governance in the different stages of the SOA lifecycle.

The final set of three papers deal with emerging concerns and domain-specific issues in service-related research. Hashmi et al. ("Normative Requirements for Business Process Compliance") address the problem of ensuring the regulatory compliance of the underlying business processes. The authors present the development and implementation of a compliance checking methodology. A preliminary evaluation of the implemented system is also included. Chen and Rabhi ("An RDR-Based Approach for Event Data Analysis") propose a useful approach to detecting event patterns using a rules learning framework called ripple-down rules (RDR) and demonstrate its capabilities based on a real-world scenario involving financial data analysis. Motamari ("A Six-Cell Services Comparison Model for Healthcare") proposes a healthcare service design framework based on a comprehensive review of the extant literature of healthcare services, especially in the context of the needs of developing countries.

April 2014

Joseph G. Davis
Haluk Demirkan
Hamid R. Motahari-Nezhad

Organization

General Chairs

Fethi Rabhi   University of New South Wales, Australia
Aditya Ghose   University of Wollongong, Australia

Program Chairs

Joseph G. Davis   University of Sydney, Australia
Haluk Demirkan   University of Washington, USA
Hamid R. Motahari-Nezhad   IBM Almaden Research Center, USA

Program Committee

Ryszard Kowalczyk   Swinburne University of Technology, Australia
Surya Nepal   CSIRO, Australia
Athman Bouguettaya   RMIT, Australia
Matti Rossi   Aalto University School of Economics, Finland
Schahram Dustdar   TU Wien, Austria
Simon Poon   University of Sydney, Australia
Babis Theodoulidis   Manchester Business School, UK
Ralph Badinelli   Virginia Tech, USA
Dragan Gasevic   Athabasca University, Canada
Yassi Moghaddam   ISSIP, USA
Hye-Young Paik   University of New South Wales, Australia
Bill Hefley   University of Pittsburgh, USA
Renu Agarwal   UTS Sydney, USA
Nirmit V. Desai   IBM Research, India
Boualem Benatallah   University of New South Wales, Australia
Charlie Bess   Hewlett Packard, USA
Albert Zomaya   University of Sydney, Australia
Byron Keating   University of Canberra, Australia
Don Allen   CISCO, USA
Alex Norta   University of Helsinki, Finland

Contents

An RDR-Based Approach for Event Data Analysis

Weisi Chen[✉] and Fethi Rabhi

School of Computer Science and Engineering,
University of New South Wales, Sydney, Australia
chenw@cse.unsw.edu.au, f.rabhi@unsw.edu.au

Abstract. Event data analysis is becoming increasingly of interest to academic researchers looking for patterns in the data, contributing to the emergence and popularity of a new field called "data intensive science". Unlike domain experts working in large companies which have access to IT staff and expensive software infrastructure, researchers find it harder to efficiently manage event processing rules by themselves especially when these rules increase in size and complexity over time. In this paper, we propose an event data analysis platform intended for non-IT experts that facilitates the evolution of event processing rules according to changing requirements. This platform integrates a rule learning framework called Ripple-Down Rules (RDR) operating in conjunction with an event pattern detection process invoked as a service. This solution is demonstrated on real-life scenario involving financial data analysis.

Keywords: Event-based data · Event processing · Event data model · Data intensive science · Ripple down rules

1   Introduction

An event is "anything that happens, or is contemplated as happening" [1] at a certain time. Examples of events in the real-world are very diverse and include financial trades and quotes, banking transactions (ATM, online, credit card use, etc.), news broadcast, aircraft movements, sensor outputs, updates in social media sites (e.g. Facebook), network communication message deliveries or computer systems management activities. We refer to large collections of event occurrences recorded in the form of data as "event data" or "event-based data". For many years, event data analysis has been conducted by the business sector for many purposes such as studying market trends, improving the efficiency of operational processes and gathering business intelligence.

To conduct event analysis tasks, domain experts have to rely on IT experts either to implement a bespoke program/service or to customize an event processing system (EPS) according to their needs. Because of constant changes in business needs and the environment, domain experts need to communicate their new requirements to IT experts all the time to update and maintain the event data analysis business logic. In terms of rule management, Luckham [2] claims that managing large sets of event processing rules is a challenge which has not yet been effectively tackled. In present

J.G. Davis et al. (Eds.): ASSRI 2013, LNBIP 177, pp. 1–14, 2014.
DOI: 10.1007/978-3-319-07950-9_1, © Springer International Publishing Switzerland 2014

event processing systems, rule sets are normally very simple. When it comes to large and complex rule sets, one typical way an event data analysis process can be supported is illustrated in Fig. 1. On the one hand, the knowledge engineer manages the rule set and on the other hand, the IT expert implements the rules according the underlying software infrastructure. There could be a multitude of domain experts defining new rules so the knowledge engineer need to constantly cooperate with IT experts to manage event processing rules particularly when the size of the rule set becomes large.

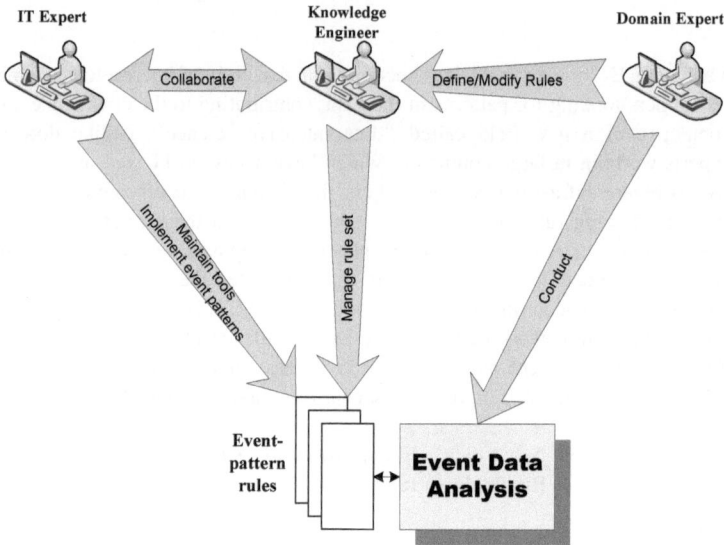

Fig. 1. Evolution of an event data analysis process.

More recently, event data analysis is becoming increasingly of interest to academic researchers looking for patterns in the data, contributing to the emergence and popularity of a new field called "data intensive science" [3]. Unlike domain experts working in large companies and having access to IT staff and expensive software infrastructures, researchers tend to conduct the analysis mostly by themselves using a range of data processing and statistical tools. Therefore, there is a need to enable analysis of event data by domain experts who have limited IT expertise and fewer resources available to them. Whilst the prime motivation of investigating solutions would be of interest to academic researchers, this research avenue would also be relevant to Small and Medium Enterprises (SMEs) looking for simple and cost-effective event data analysis solutions.

In this paper, we propose an approach to enable domain experts to manage event data analysis with little or no IT expert intervention by:

• Integrating a rule learning framework supporting incremental acquisition that enables domain users to define and add rules by themselves;

- Providing event pattern detection as a service (EPDaaS) in a way that allows domain users to conduct event processing without the concern about which event processing language/engine to use.

The rest of the paper is organized as follows. In Sect. 2, we summarize the related research efforts on event data analysis. Section 3 explains our proposed approach. In Sect. 4, we apply our approach to a real-life case study – data cleansing on financial data – to validate our proposed architecture. Section 5 concludes the paper and presents the direction of our future work.

2 Background

2.1 Basic Assumptions

There are several unique characteristics of event data; the primary ones are as follows:

- Time-based: Event data represent or record events, flowing in time-streams. Compared with normal data, event data has a temporal axis in the data schema. To be precise, every event data record is affixed with a timestamp as well as other attributes when it is created. Due to this feature, an event database can also be called time-series database.
- High flow rate and huge volume: Normally, new event data is continuously coming in to guarantee the timeliness of the data. Also, event data records are generated and stored in huge volumes, containing data for years.
- Immutable: On account of the high flow rate of event data, each record comes in and will never be modified.
- Referable: Any event record may be relevant to previous records and can be referred to other relevant records on some conditions such as within a certain time window, several days before or after the current event, etc.
- Influential: Any new event may generate a bunch of new events. For instance, financial market event data represent stimuli, market state transitions and outputs, each of which is issued followed by a chain of responses such as state changes and new outputs.

We view event data analysis as primarily the process of detecting patterns in the data and taking a number of actions accordingly. An example is described next followed by a review of existing work in this area.

2.2 Motivating Example

This example involves the analysis of Sirca's daily data [4] by academic researchers. Often, financial time-series analysis requires the computation of a company returns over a period of time. However, the value of these returns is affected by corporate actions such as the issuing of dividends. A dividend denotes a payment made by a firm out of its current or accumulated retained earnings to its owners, which gives rise to a fall of the stock price by the dividend amount on the executive date. Although the information on corporate actions is available in the data, processing it is a non-trivial task due to the need to deal with duplicate dividend announcement records. Table 1 illustrates different cases for handling this problem. In most cases (e.g. Table 1(a)), duplicate events are just recording the same dividend announcement for multiple times. The initial logic of duplicate dividend detection is:

If there are two Dividend events issued at the same event time (Date)
　　Then it is a duplicate so delete the first one

After a while, domain users may find this logic gives wrong decisions and actions in a new case (e.g. Table 1(b)), so they have to change the rule into:

If there are two Dividend events with the same event time (Date) and Div ID
　　Then it is a duplicate so delete the first one

Soon later, due to another new case (e.g. Table 1(c)), this rule has to be again modified into:

If there are two Dividend events with the same event time, the same Div ID, and the payment status of these two events are both marked 'approved' ('APPD'), and the values of 'Div Delete Marker' are both 0
　　Then it is a duplicate so delete the first one

Table 1. Different cases in duplicate dividend detection

(a) Case 1 – simple duplicate dividend records

#RIC	Date	Type	Div Ex Date	Div Amt	Div ID	Div Delete Marker	Payment Status
ABC	12/08/2012	Dividend	11/09/2012	0.07	7885540	0	APPD
ABC	12/08/2012	Dividend	11/09/2012	0.07	7885540	0	APPD

(b) Case 2 –although these two dividends are issued at the same time (Date), the Div IDs are different which indicates that these are two different dividends rather than a duplicate.

#RIC	Date	Type	Div Ex Date	Div Amt	Div ID	Div Delete Marker	Payment Status
ABC	12/08/2012	Dividend	11/09/2012	0.07	7885540	0	APPD
ABC	12/08/2012	Dividend	11/10/2012	0.07	7926058	0	APPD

(c) Case 3 –the first dividend is proposed (PROP) and has been deleted (Delete Marker = 1), which is considered to be an out-dated record; the second dividend is an update so this case is not a case of a "duplicate dividend„ to be detected.

#RIC	Date	Type	Div Ex Date	Div Amt	Div ID	Div Delete Marker	Payment Status
ABC	12/08/2012	Dividend	11/09/2012	0.08	7885540	1	PROP
ABC	12/08/2012	Dividend	11/09/2012	0.07	7885540	0	APPD

In real-world event processing, rules are never "perfect" as there are always exceptions against existing rules. As an extension of the example above, the defined data cleansing rules built for Australian stock data may be applied to other country's stock data, e.g. the German stock data, with similar but not exactly the same logic, which requires additional modifications to the rules which can be even more complicated than the example above. This also explains why IT experts and knowledge engineers are always needed to evolve the program or system; in many cases, they have to develop a number of various applications for different or even slightly different event processing tasks.

2.3 Related Work

According to the book **Event Processing in Action** [5], event processing is "computing that performs operations on events". The main operations on events include:

- Filter: reducing the overall set of events to be processed by an event-processing system to those events that are actually relevant for the given processing task, e.g., removing erroneous or incomplete data.
- Transformation: changing event instances from one form to another, including translation, splitting, aggregation, composition, etc.
- Pattern Detection: finding a particular pattern by examining a collection of events.

An event processing system is typically a dedicated platform that provides abstractions (event processing logic) for operations on events that are separated from the application logic (event producers and event consumers). This can reduce the cost of development and maintenance. Event processing logic is expressed by event processing languages (EPLs). A stream of event data is fed into the EPS and the event processing language code is executed, then a list of actions is generated (Fig. 2). Table 2 lists different types of event processing languages. These languages all have advantages and disadvantages that reflect the usual tradeoffs between simplicity and expressiveness. Therefore, whatever EPL/EPS the domain user uses, there might always be limitations, and switching is by any means troublesome. This is to say that the performance of the event data analysis largely depends on the selected EPL/EPS.

In the book **The Power of Events** [1], Luckham have defined event processing rules as "the foundation for applications of complex event processing (CEP)". Although some work has realized that user customization of the system according to

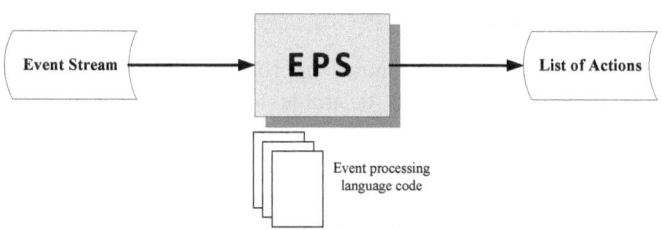

Fig. 2. An event data analysis process.

Table 2. Types and examples of event processing languages

Language type		Language/product [5, 6]
Stream-oriented (SQL extension)		Aleri, Esper, CQL
Rule-oriented	Production rules	DROOLS fusion, TIBCO BusinessEvents
	ECA rules	Amit, IBM WebSphere Business Events
	Logic programming	Etails, Prova
Imperative		MonitorScript, Netcool Impact policy language
Event processing framework or library for a general purpose programming language		Progress Apama

their needs is an important criterion for EPS [7], most efforts are focusing on the operational issues, e.g. event processing language expressiveness and performance [8], rather than event processing rule management. Most work on EPS does not support user-driven event data analysis no matter how good the language expressivity is. Among the very limited discussion on event processing rule management, there are two important insights:

- Reuse of existing event patterns is of great importance for efficiency [9].
- The idea of rule templates are suitable for EPS for completing rules as well as decoupled "building blocks" of rule logic [10].

We agree with these insights. However, the use of rule templates is not sufficient to eliminate rule re-building efforts when modifying the rule. In most cases, the same IT expert and/or knowledge engineer who built the existing rule set (rule base) are needed to re-build the entire rule set. Besides, most literature on event processing rule management tends to focus on building each single rule and disregard the management of the rule base as a whole. It has been proved in the knowledge acquisition community that when the size of the rule base becomes huge, it would be very difficult to maintain the rule base, as any modification of the rule base may cause the system collapse [11]. Thus in most existing EPSs, as rules may be closely associated with each other, it is difficult to keep track of changes effectively.

3 Proposed System

3.1 Architecture

In this paper, we are proposing a novel approach to facilitate incremental event processing rule definition, which is desirable to eliminate event processing rule-rebuilding, to enhance the reuse of existing event processing rules, to keep track of event processing changes, to simplify rule management process, and to avoid rule base collapse. Our architecture enables domain experts to manage rules, define simple event patterns or build event patterns upon existing ones. In addition, the event data analysis system can be incrementally enhanced by domain users. In this case, IT experts will only play one role in the data analysis process: to define and deploy complex event patterns.

The proposed architecture illustrated in Fig. 3 has two components – a rule-based system and an event pattern detection as a service (EPDaaS). In order to achieve "incremental management" and eliminate clashes, we utilize a framework called Ripple Down Rules (RDR) in the rule-based system to route the event processing logic, which can organize and maintain the rule base more effectively [11]. Unlike other rule management systems, RDR is an error-driven, incremental rule acquisition framework, which enables domain experts to evolve the system solely by themselves and eliminates the risk of corrupting the rule base because all existing rules are never changed, which reserve the existing decision logic of the event processing. When errors occur, RDR allows users to capture the characteristic of the new case as an "exception", and add a new rule to quickly recover the degraded performance. The case that prompted the addition of a rule is called a cornerstone case, which is stored along with the rule and is used to be compared with new cases by the domain experts. It has been proved that the whole processing of adding a rule including checking cornerstone cases takes only a couple of minutes [12].

In this architecture, the EPDaaS has a service interface that has the ability to invoke any underlying EPS (using any EPL) to detect event patterns. When invoked with an event pattern type and a reference to an event stream, EPDaaS will select one available/suitable EPS, run the corresponding EPL code and finally return event pattern occurrences in this event stream, abstractions or aggregations of these

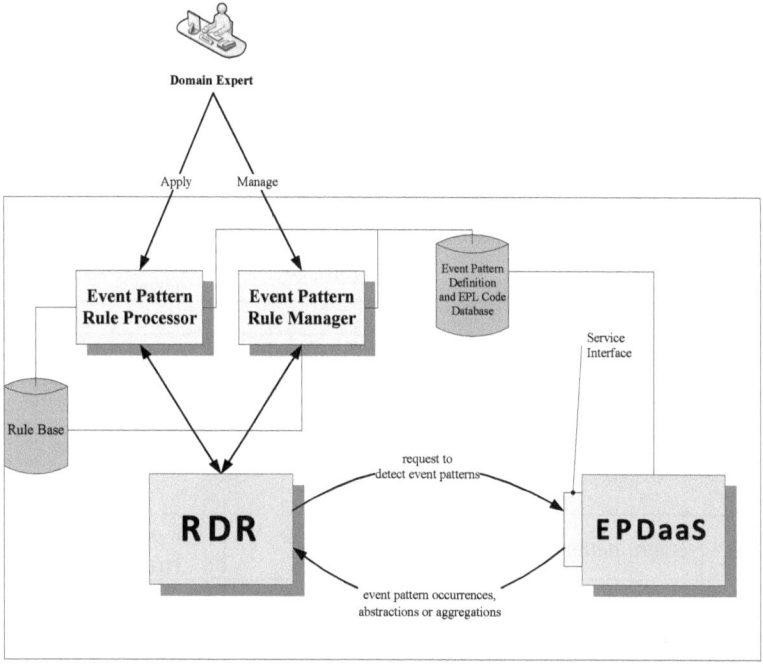

Fig. 3. Proposed EP-RDR architecture

occurrences. The role of the RDR component is to allow incremental definition of rules based on the presence of event patterns – each event "situation" is represented as an event pattern in a rule. The architecture provides the link between the RDR and the EPDaaS components, i.e. the RDR component sends a request to detect an event pattern, and the EPDaaS responds with event pattern occurrences back to the RDR. Finally, RDR will generate a list of actions on the original event stream, which will be inspected by the domain expert. One of the advantages of this architecture is that for different event data analysis, the only things that have to be changed are the rule set and the choice of the EPS invoked by the EPDaaS component; the RDR component, however, does not have to be changed. IT experts are not involved in rule management but managing the EPL code in the database. We call this architecture Event-Processing RDR (EP-RDR).

3.2   Overview of Event Processing Rules

Generally, an event processing RDR rule can be:

     If
          *an **event pattern** occurs*
     Then
          case action;
          *inference action: go to rule **a***
     Else
          *inference action: go to rule **b***

If an error is found in a new case, domain experts can use the Event Pattern Rule Manager to associate a new event-based rule to the rule that causes the error. Table 3 illustrates the evolution of duplicate dividend rule in EP-RDR. Table 3(a) is a sample of the initial rule set, in which Rule 4 handles a duplicate dividend case in Table 1(a). The domain user executes this rule set and finds out an error occurs on Rule 4 due to

Table 3. (a) A sample of the original rule base for event data cleansing. (b) The evolved sample of rule base for event data cleansing.

(a)

Rule No.	Event pattern ID	Action	Inf. action (true)	Inf. action (false)
...	...	...	...	...
4	4	Delete duplicate Div	to rule 5	to rule 5
...	...	...	...	...
7	7	Report it as an error	exit	exit

(b)

Rule No.	Event pattern ID	Action	Inf. action (true)	Inf. action (false)
...	...	...	...	...
4	4	Delete duplicate Div	to rule *8*	to rule 5
...	...	...	...	...
7	7	Report it as an error	exit	exit
8	*8*	*Retrieve the last action*	to rule *5*	to rule *5*

the case in Table 1(b); then the domain user can add a new rule (Rule 8) to take the attribute *Div ID* into account. The new rule is attached to Rule 4, whose Inf. action (true) is modified (Table 3(b)). Also, the case in Table 1(b) – the cornerstone case – is stored together with Rule 8. Table 4 shows a summary of the event pattern types used in this example.

Table 4. Event pattern types used in rule base example

Event pattern ID	Event pattern definition
4	Another dividend event is before the current dividend with the same date
7	Missing an End Of Day event on the effective date of a capital change event
8	*Two dividend events have different Div ID*

Figure 4 illustrates how an event processing rule is added. Before defining a rule, an event pattern must be newly defined or selected from the pre-existing event patterns via an event pattern definition GUI. Note that every time a new pattern is defined, it is saved so that all defined event patterns can be re-used when building new rules. After defining or selecting the event pattern, the domain expert can use a rule definition GUI to define the rule and associate the pattern with the condition and action of the rule.

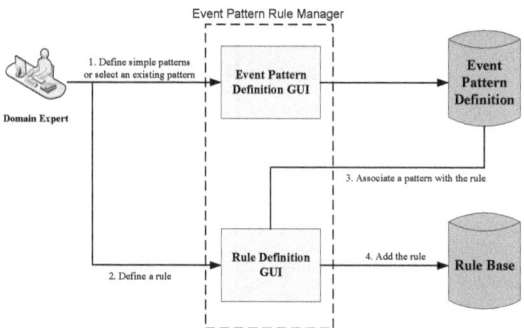

Fig. 4. Event processing rule management.

3.3 A Dynamic View of EP-RDR

Figure 5 demonstrates the business process associated with event-pattern RDR rule execution. For each single rule being processed on an event, the RDR engine sends a request to the EPDaaS with three inputs:

- (1) the key of the event pattern to be detected (the key is used as an index in the event pattern definition and EPL code database);
- (2) a reference to the event stream to be searched from, along with a reference event to be used as the original point to detect the particular event pattern occurrence(s).

For each occurrence sent back by EPDaaS, RDR will then assert the action according to the rule and go to the next rule according to the inference defined in the rule. After processing all rules on all events, a log with a list of actions and a track of

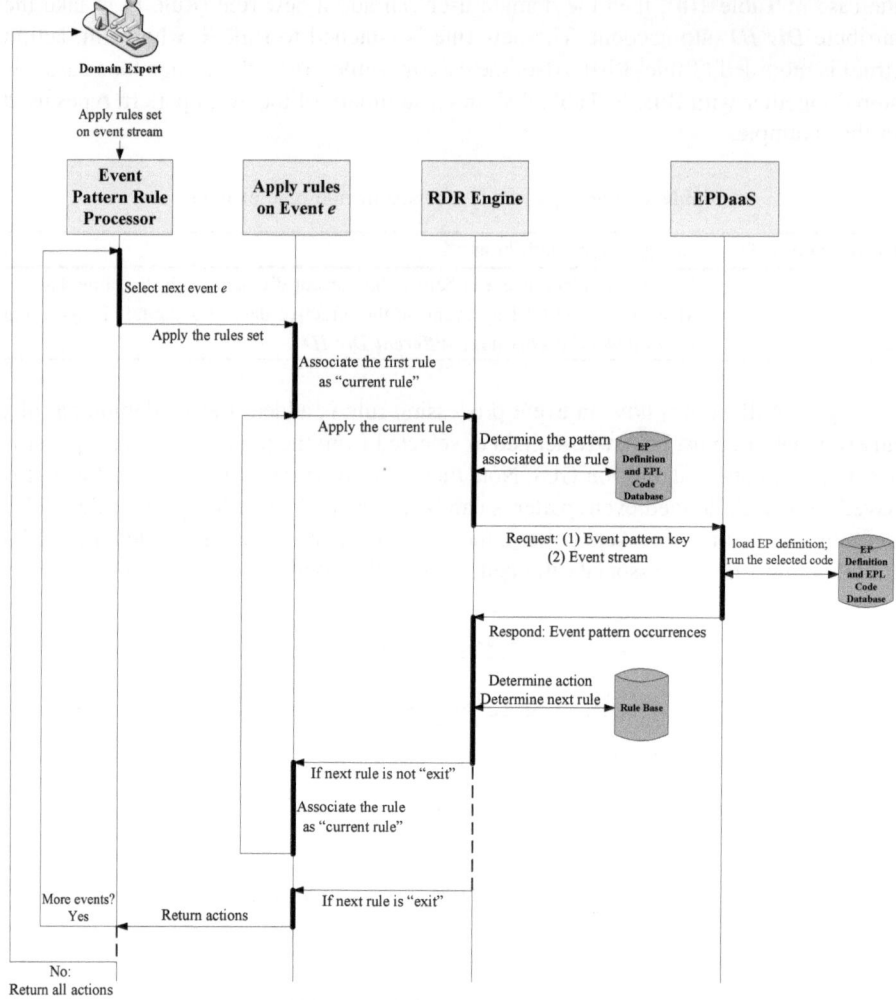

Fig. 5. Apply rules on events.

all "decisions" made during execution will be generated for the domain expert's inspection. Figure 6 shows what the domain expert has to do after the rule execution process: inspect the result; if an error is found due to a case, the domain expert can add a new rule, where the cornerstone case is stored.

To enable communication between the RDR engine and the EPDaaS, we have designed a new event data model (see Fig. 7), which allows the architecture to be independent from any particular event processing language.

There are two sub-types of events, i.e. simple events and complex events. A complex event is generated by an event pattern occurrence that matches a particular event pattern. Each event pattern occurrence involves a number of events, which can be simple events as well as complex events. All events have a number of attributes

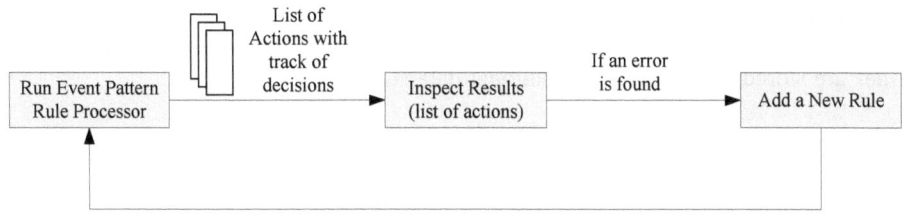

Fig. 6. Rule evolution.

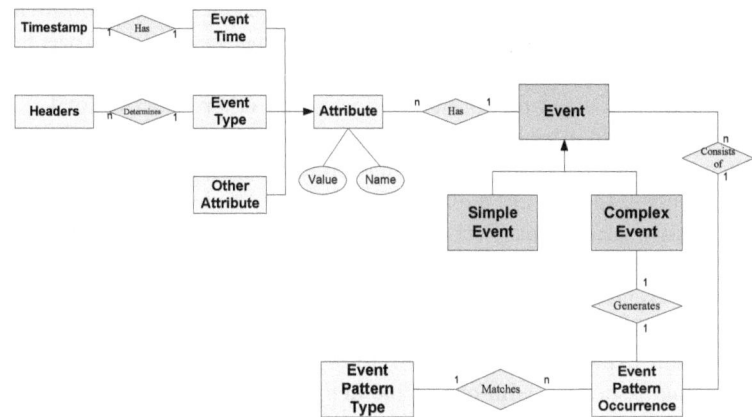

Fig. 7. Event data model.

including "event time" that has a timestamp and "event type" that determines the headers of attributes. For more details about this data model, see [13].

4   Application and Validation

4.1   Implementation

We have implemented a prototype of the proposed architecture in Java with a simple GUI which allows users to define RDR rules as well as simple event pattern types graphically (using JGraph). In this prototype, the underlying event pattern rule processor is a Java program that implements the rule processing logic. Among many structures of RDR, rather than using a tree structure in most RDR applications [14, 15], we apply the linked-production structure, where all rules are at the same level and can be reused. Therefore, event processing logic is separated from the inference logic, and modifications can be made merely on inference logic (which rule to be processed next) rather than on the content of rules (event patterns or actions) when adding rules. This method can reduce rule redundancy and protect existing rules for the sake of rule maintenance. The example previously shown in Table 3 essentially uses the linked-production RDR structure.

The EPDaaS used in this prototype is also a dedicated Java program that implements some simple pattern detection functions. All event pattern definitions/code and rules are stored in PostgreSQL relational database separately.

4.2   Case Study – Event Data Cleansing

Due to its unique characteristics listed in Sect. 2.1, event data cleansing is an important part of event data analysis. Working with a domain expert in the financial area, the case study involves conducting data cleansing in the context of Sirca daily stock data. As preliminary work, we developed a bespoke program which implemented the data cleansing process. However, every time the domain expert has asked for the business logic to be changed, it took several days to modify the program, as changes on one particular rule normally affect some other rules. In total, 8 modifications took more than a year to complete.

We then repeated the process using the prototype. Firstly, we defined 7 initial event patterns using the Event Pattern Definition GUI, each representing one type of event data quality issue respectively: missing value in an end-of-day (EOD) event, missing value in a dividend (Div) event, missing value in a capital change (CC) event, duplicate Div events, duplicate CC events, missing an EOD event on dividend effective date (DED), missing an EOD event on capital change effective date (CCED). Then the domain expert defined totally 7 rules (Table 5) using the Rule Definition GUI, each being associated with one of the defined event patterns.

The domain expert worked iteratively by executing the current rule set, inspecting the resulting list of generated actions and decisions, and adding new rules. Table 6 shows the rule base after the 8 iterations, which only took several hours. The performance is as good as the bespoke program. Note that at each stage of the evolution, each existing rule is true in terms of all previously encountered cases. Compared to the previous approach, the domain expert was able to update the rule base simply and neatly without assistance by the IT expert with significantly less amount of time.

Table 5. Initial data cleansing rule set

Rule no.	Event pattern	Action	Inf. action (true)	Inf. action (false)
1	Missing value in an EOD event	Fill in with previous value	To rule 2	To rule 2
2	Missing value in a Div event	Report missing value	To rule 3	To rule 3
3	Missing value in a CC event	Report missing value	To rule 4	To rule 4
4	Duplicate Div events	Delete the former one	To rule 5	To rule 5
5	Duplicate CC events	Delete the former one	To rule 6	To rule 6
6	Missing an EOD event on DED	Report it as an error	To rule 7	To rule 7
7	Missing an EOD event on CCED	Report it as an error	Exit	Exit

Table 6. Evolved data cleansing rule set

Rule no.	Event pattern	Action	Inf. action (true)	Inf. action (false)
1	Missing value in an EOD event	Fill in with previous value	To rule 2	To rule 2
2	Missing value in a Div event	Report missing value	To rule 3	To rule 3
3	Missing value in a CC event	Report missing value	To rule 4	To rule 4
4	Duplicate Div events	Delete the former one	To rule *8*	To rule 5
5	Duplicate CC events	Delete the former one	To rule *11*	To rule 6
6	Missing an EOD event on DED	Report it as an error	To rule 7	To rule *14*
7	Missing an EOD event on CCED	Report it as an error	Exit	To rule *15*
8	Different Div ID	*Retrieve the last action*	To rule 5	To rule *9*
9	Status is not "APPD"	*Retrieve the last action*	To rule 5	To rule *10*
10	Delete Marker is not 0	*Retrieve the last action*	To rule 5	To rule 5
11	Different CC ID	*Retrieve the last action*	To rule 6	To rule *12*
12	Status is not "APPD"	*Retrieve the last action*	To rule 6	To rule *13*
13	Delete Marker is not 0	*Retrieve the last action*	To rule 6	To rule 6
14	There is a corresponding EOD event but no trading	*Report it as an error*	To rule *7*	To rule *7*
15	There is a corresponding EOD event but no trading	*Report it as an error*	Exit	Exit

5   Conclusion and Future Work

In this paper, we have proposed an architecture called EP-RDR for building and maintaining user-driven event data analysis, in which a Ripple-Down Rule (RDR) framework is integrated with an event pattern detection service. Our architecture is designed to optimize the process of rule management from the perspective of managing the whole rule base and to leverage the power of existing Event Processing Systems.

We have implemented a prototype of the architecture, and validated the architecture by applying it to event data cleansing in the context of Sirca daily stock data. The implementation has proved successful in evolving 15 rules, which is not a very huge rule base size. Besides, the implementation has been validated with financial data, even though potentially most event data analysis in other domains can be defined and maintained easily with the proposed architecture. In our future research, we will focus on managing larger rule bases and apply the approach in various domains.

Acknowledgement. We would like to thank the Smart Services Cooperative Research Centre in Australia for sponsoring our research project and Sirca for providing financial data used in the case study. We would also thank Prof. Paul Compton for his valuable advice on the RDR technique.

References

1. Luckham, D.: The Power of Events: An Introduction to Complex Event Processing in Distributed Enterprise Systems. Addison Wesley Professional, Reading (2002)

2. Luckham, D.: What's the Difference Between ESP and CEP? (2006). http://www.complexevents.com/?p=103

3. Rabhi, F., Yao, L., Guabtni, A.: ADAGE: a framework for supporting user-driven ad hoc data analysis processes. Computing **94**, 489–519 (2012)

4. Sirca. http://www.sirca.org.au/

5. Etzion, O., Niblett, P.: Event Processing in Action. Manning Publications Co., Stamford (2011)

6. Cugola, G., Margara, A.: Processing flows of information: from data stream to complex event processing. ACM Comput. Surv. **44**, 1–62 (2012)

7. Chandy, K., Schulte, W.: Event Processing: Designing IT Systems for Agile Companies. McGraw-Hill, New York (2010)

8. Hinze, A., Sachs, K., Buchmann, A.: Event-based applications and enabling technologies. In: Proceedings of the Third ACM International Conference on Distributed Event-Based Systems, Nashville, Tennessee (2009)

9. Sen, S., Stojanovic, N.: GRUVe: a methodology for complex event pattern life cycle management. In: Pernici, B. (ed.) CAiSE 2010. LNCS, vol. 6051, pp. 209–223. Springer, Heidelberg (2010)

10. Obweger, H., Schiefer, J., Suntinger, M., Kepplinger, P., Rozsnyai, S.: User-Oriented Rule Management for Event-Based Applications. In: Proceedings of the Fifth ACM International Conference on Distributed Event-Based System, New York, USA (2011)

11. Richards, D.: Two decades of ripple down rules research. Knowl. Eng. Rev. **24**(2), 159–184 (2009)

12. Compton, P., Peters, L., Edwards, G., Lavers, T.G.: Experience with ripple-down rules. Knowl. Based Syst. **19**, 356–362 (2006)

13. Rabhi, F.A., Chen, W., Perry, R., Yao, L., Natarajan A.: A new data model for representing events and event patterns. Internal Report, Service Oriented Computing Research Group, School of Computer Science and Engineering, University of New South Wales (2013)

14. Kang, B.H., Compton, P., Preston, P.: Multiple classification ripple down rules: evaluation and possibilities. In: The Ninth Banff Knowledge Acquisition for Knowledge Based Systems Workshop (1995)

15. Prasad, K.H., Faruquie, T.A., Joshi, S., Chaturvedi, S., Subramaniam, L.V., Mohania M.: Data cleansing techniques for large enterprise datasets. In: Annual SRII Global Conference (SRII), pp. 135–144 (2011)

Effective Governance During SOA Lifecycle - Theory and Practice

George Joukhadar[1](✉) and Fethi Rabhi[2]

[1] School of Information Systems, Technology and Management,
University of New South Wales, Sydney, Australia
g.joukhadar@student.unsw.edu.au
[2] School of Computer Science and Engineering,
University of New South Wales, Sydney, Australia
f.rabhi@unsw.edu.au

Abstract. This research provides a theoretical conceptualization of SOA governance aspects that can be used to assess SOA governance practices and provide guidance to improve them. The review of IT and SOA governance shows that there are conflicting claims and inconsistency in the literature concerning the role of SOA governance. Moreover, there is no empirical evidence on the implications of the governance frameworks used for SOA and how they are working in the most effective ways. As a result, there is confusion in practice as the issues of SOA governance have not been successfully addressed. Based on an extensive analysis of major governance frameworks, a comprehensive list of key SOA governance aspects is proposed. This research will focus on the assessment of the importance of SOA governance aspects by finding the role of the governance framework during the different activities of SOA lifecycle and outlining the discrepancies between theory and practice.

Keywords: Service-oriented · IT governance · SOA governance · SOA governance model · Governance aspects · Governance processes · Service lifecycle

1 Introduction

Service Oriented Architecture (SOA) governance has become a topic of high interest for both academics and practitioners. While the academic literature is focusing on the technical aspects associated of SOA [1, 2] and the major software vendors are putting huge efforts to promote the growth of SOA adoption [1], there has been a lack of empirical evidence about SOA governance and SOA governance models. CIOs are recognizing the need to align business and IT in meaningful and measurable ways [3, 4]. However, no common understanding of SOA governance exists [5]. This research focuses on drawing the main aspects of SOA governance from previous work and examines the role of these aspects in building effective SOA governance.

Section 2 of this paper provides a literature review on the major aspects of SOA governance. Section 3 discusses the research approach, methodology and design used to achieve the aims of this study while Sects. 4 and 5 address the preliminary results and future work respectively.

J.G. Davis et al. (Eds.): ASSRI 2013, LNBIP 177, pp. 15–28, 2014.
DOI: 10.1007/978-3-319-07950-9_2, © Springer International Publishing Switzerland 2014

2 Literature Review

2.1 SOA Governance Standards

The difference between SOA and IT architectures is its emphasis on Information Systems (IS) agility which enhances business agility [6]. Unlike other architectures, the SOA paradigm creates an IT view from a business process perspective. It allows these business processes to be constructed, analyzed, and modified much more easily [7].

Researchers agree that organizations planning to broadly adopt SOA should start with governance [8–13]. Organizations need to decide how to implement governance over the SOA implementation in the organization. Technology adoption alone is not enough to enable business or IT transformation [4] - for the fact that decisions made in the information system affect and are affected by the impact that IT has on business processes [14]. When organizations choose to treat integration as just another technology implementation, experiences show zero to minimal reuse, minimal improvement in business responsiveness or flexibility, and higher IT costs over time [4]. Therefore, we see that SOA governance is extending out of IT and merging with business considerations [15]. This comprehensive SOA governance will provide additional strength to the overall information management policies, and aid in maintaining the authenticity and integrity of the corporate information assets [16].

In order to address the existing challenges and successful SOA adoption, organizations need exact definition of processes and relationships, control mechanisms, SOA metrics and enforcement of policies that are defined in an SOA governance framework. The role of an SOA governance framework is defining the set of processes, organization structures, policies, solutions and technologies that can help to manage complex SOA deployment in an effective and efficient manner [17].

2.2 SOA Governance Framework Aspects

There is a general consensus in the literature that there are many different aspects of SOA governance. These aspects vary across different authors and vendors. To identify the existing SOA governance aspects, an extensive literature review on major IT and SOA governance frameworks has been conducted.

Review of Major IT Governance Frameworks

The IT Infrastructure Library (ITIL) mainly deals with IT process definition [12]. It supports implementation of processes related to delivery and support of IT and details establishment and maintenance of service level agreements and operation level agreements.

The basis of COBIT is that accountability of the IT systems is achieved by the use of a set of audit control processes [18]. The framework provides a definition of IT governance consisting of four domains and 34 processes. Each process contains a number of IT governance maturity indicators, such as activities, documents, metrics, and support for role and responsibility assignment. These 34 reference processes are defined as control framework, more tightly aligned with the business objectives of the organization than with operational issues [12, 19].

Val IT takes IT governance onto a higher level of abstraction by providing general directions on how to manage IT from a business point of view. The high level of abstraction is however also a limitation, as Val IT purely focuses on the interface between IT and the business and lacks the support to represent e.g. the processes of an IT organization [20]. Val IT takes on where COBIT ends, and the two frameworks complement each other well [21].

While COBIT processes manage all IT related activities and Val IT best describes how to progress and maximize the return on investment, the role of Risk IT is enhance risk management. Risk IT was published in 2009 by ISACA [22]. It is the result of a work group composed by industry experts and some academics of different nations, coming from organizations such as IBM, PricewaterhouseCoopers, Risk Management Insight, Swiss Life, and KPMG. Risk IT is a framework based on a set of guiding principles for effective management of IT risk [22].

The COBIT 5 framework is the successor to the COBIT 4.1, with the Risk IT and Val IT frameworks integrated as well. Where principles, policies, frameworks, culture, ethics and behaviour were mentioned in a few COBIT 4.1 processes, COBIT 5 is based on a revised process reference model with a new governance domain and several new and modified processes that now cover enterprise activities end-to-end, i.e., business and IT function areas. COBIT 5 consolidates COBIT 4.1, Val IT and Risk IT into one framework, and has been updated to align with current best practices, e.g. ITIL [23].

Weill and Ross [24] have identified six interacting components for the effective design of IT Governance in their framework. Their main focus lies in the use of IT metrics and accountabilities to influence behaviour. The goal is to create target-oriented incentives in order to evoke specific desirable behaviour. However, their model does not cover SOA lifecycle [12].

SOA Governance Frameworks Proposed in the Research Literature
Numerous models for SOA Governance have been proposed so far. Most of them are motivated by software providers that offer SOA business solutions and closely align their SOA governance perspectives with their products [12]. They differ extensively in scope and capability and many remain abstract. They emphasize on different aspects, e.g., service lifecycle management or organizational change.

Bieberstein et al. [25] propose an SOA Governance Model in which they identify six governance processes and three steps for launching the SOA governance model. They found that SOA strategy and SOA objectives should be defined in such a way that both the business and IT units have a clear understanding of such objectives. Accordingly, policies defined by governance positions should form the basis for any decision. Their model is made complete by a set of best practices.

Derler and Weinreich [26] propose a framework that deals mainly with services. They looked at the governance issues from a technical side. They provided two main tools: the Service Repository Console and the Service Browser. They stated that their model is to support service reuse and service lifecycle activities.

Kuang-Yu et al. [27] developed their own framework because they could not find any suitable on the market that could meet their special requirements for Chunghwa Telecom (CHT). The main functions of their system which they called Service Oriented Bus (SOBUS) are: (1) Managing the applications and registrations of the services on Enterprise Service Bus (ESB). (2) Managing and monitoring the web services and messages services. (3) Analysis of services performance.

Varadan et al. [4] enlightened in their framework on the added benefits of an SOA documented vision and how it can drive the scope towards an SOA governance. They cited four governance processes that must be included in the framework: compliance, vitality, exceptions and appeals and communication. They argued that the use of Enterprise Service Bus is essential for SOA adoption and how using it with a registry can increase business benefits.

Neimann et al. [12, 28] propose an SOA governance framework that consists of two parts: the SOA Governance Control Cycle and the SOA Governance Operational model. According to them, the first represents the overall steering process that controls the operation of the SOA system and it consists of four phases: planning, design, realization and operation. The operational model describes the activities and competencies. They argued that the two parts interact with each other.

de Leusse et al. [29] propose an SOA governance framework based on requirements that underline the need for policy and process management, policy administration, resource life-cycle management, resource adaptation, resource visibility and resource contextualization. They made a distinction between the operational, data and management models. In the operational model, they listed: business capability, infrastructure capability, access control, identity management, message interceptor, metadata repository, policy management, profile management and service registry. In the Object model, they listed the policies and processes. In the management model, they listed profile management, capability management and governance layer base.

Hojaji and Shirazi [17, 30, 31], developed an SOA governance framework based on COBIT 4.1. Their framework consists of a set of service lifecycle processes governed by governance processes. They stated that their framework contributes to SOA governance needs by: promoting the alignment of business and IT, organizing service lifecycle and governance processes, defining the management control objectives, providing SOA reference architecture and infrastructure, and providing metrics and maturity models to measure achievement of defined goals.

Vendor-Based SOA Governance Frameworks

The SOA governance approach proposed by Oracle consists of nine 'key areas of interest', that are combined with a structured set of best practices. It is completed by an SOA adaptation model which defines a cycle of six steps that supports continuous improvement of the SOA [32].

Software AG [8] identifies maturity and governance levels. Their maturity model is consisted of six levels and they also defined an SOA service lifecycle which incorporates services, artifacts and roles. They provided a five-step SOA adaptation plan and a set of best practices [28].

Before being acquired by Software AG in 2007, the SOA governance approach at WebMethods consists of two parts: Architecture Governance and Service Lifecycle

Governance. The latter is divided into design-time, run-time and change-time Governance. Architecture Governance deals with issues such as corporate technology standards, the definition of an SOA topology and the determination of an SOA platform strategy. Service Lifecycle Governance focuses on the regulation of design, etc. of services through its respective policies and enforcement mechanisms [28, 33].

Authors at IBM - have defined SOA Governance as an extension of IT Governance that focuses on the service lifecycle and composite applications [28]. The IBM SOA Governance model comprises a service lifecycle and an SOA governance lifecycle, both consist of four phases [34–36]. They also advocated a best practice approach for performing SOA governance called SOA Governance and Management Method (SGMM). SGMM focuses on the three main aspects: people (including governance organizational structures and the concept of a Center of Excellence), process (the governance processes used to govern the SOA) and technology. The SGMM reference model defines concepts in terms of principles, organizations roles and responsibilities, infrastructure and tools, and governing and governed processes.

In conclusion there are many IT and SOA governance frameworks, either proposed or vendor-based. The next section will show which aspects are recognized by each of frameworks reviewed above.

2.3   Summary of SOA Governance Aspects

Based on an extensive analysis of governance frameworks described above, a comprehensive list of key SOA governance aspects is proposed. This paragraph will define each of these aspects, set them up in a table to compare them against different proposed frameworks, and discuss the research issues. The aspects could be classified into the followings two categories:

SOA Business Aspects

- SOA vision: This element shows to which degree implementing an SOA governance model can provide a clear SOA vision for the enterprise. Its role is to make sure SOA is compliant with the governed processes.
- SOA roadmap: Is one of the most important aspects of the framework; its major role is in the Planning phase as well defining an 'SOA Strategy Plan process' [17].
- SOA maturity: Is a method of evaluating the organization that creates an understanding of the maturity level of SOA within the organization and its readiness to ensure that framework is defined in an appropriate level for the organization [30].
- Service lifecycle management: Is the key component of an SOA governance framework [37]. It includes the processes to produce and manage services. It comprises main processes to design, develop, deploy, manage and retire services [30].
- Service Portfolio Management: Is the main process of the service strategy involved determinant control objectives and measurement metrics [17].
- SOA Business capabilities: When implementing SOA organizations should be able to realize business capabilities to gain increased visibility across the IT landscape.

- Governance processes: Includes the governance processes to manage service life-cycle activities.
- Organizational change management: Companies that build strong SOA governance and change management capabilities — in tandem with their SOA technology and processes — are poised to reap significant improvements in business agility and speed to market [38].
- SOA Governance Board (or Centre of Excellence - CoE): This is referred to the board of people who govern SOA.
- Open service market-place management: The governance framework should go over geographical boundaries [12].

SOA Technical Aspects

- Enterprise Service Bus (ESB): The Enterprise Service Bus role is to simplify the integration of business components using a standards-based, service-oriented architecture.
- Service performance analysis: This includes the cost to build a new service, elapsed time to build a new service, service utilization, cost to run the service, governance costs and mainly Return on Investment (ROI).
- Policy management: This is the role of the governance Board or (Centre of Excellence). Policies should define clearly the role and responsibility of who will manage, change, and use the service.
- Best practices deployment: Organizations should use best practices and guidance related to SOA and service management especially for determining control objectives and measurement metrics [17].
- SOA Governance Technology: Controls and policies should be introduced enforced in the SOA service lifecycle [17].
- Infrastructure capability: Organizations need to assure that their infrastructure is ready to launch a service.
- Process monitoring and evaluation: is being considered part of the governance lifecycle and the service operation of the service lifecycle [17].
- Service transparency control: Through the registration and discovery mechanism, SOA should provide service location transparency, which allows clients not to know about where a component or service is actually located.
- Service security control: Organizations need to assure their services are secure enough to use.

Table 1 classifies the SOA governance aspects and shows how these aspects are addressed by the IT and SOA governance frameworks discussed previously.

In conclusion, there is no empirical evidence on the implications of the governance frameworks used for SOA and how these frameworks are actually working in the most effective way. There is so much that is not known and not researched and there are many claims made in the literature that are not substantiated by empirical evidence. As a result there is confusion about the usage of SOA governance, and hence the aspects of SOA governance have not been successfully addressed.

Table 1. SOA governance aspects

Table 1 – SOA Governance Aspects

Vendors				Proposed SOA Gov							IT Gov						Frameworks categories
IBM	WebMethods	SoftwareAG	Oracle	(Hojaji and Shirazi, 2010b)	(Varadan et al., 2008)	(de Leusse et al., 2009)	(Niemann et al., 2008)	(Kuang-Yu et al., 2008)	(Derler and Weinreich, 2007)	(Bieberstein et al., 2006)	COBIT 5	RiskIT	ValIT	COBIT 4.1	ITIL	Weill/Ross	Framework — SOA Aspects
																	SOA Governance Business Aspects
																	SOA vision
																	SOA roadmap
																	Centre of Excellence (CoE)
																	SOA Maturity
																	Service lifecycle management
																	SOA Business capabilities
																	Governance processes
																	Organizational changes
																	Service Portfolio management
																	Open service market-place
																	SOA Governance Technical Aspects
																	Enterprise Service Bus (ESB)
																	Service performance analysis
																	Policy management
																	Best Practices deployment
																	SOA Governance Technology
																	Infrastructure capability
																	Process monitoring & evaluation
																	Service transparency control
																	Service security control

Legend:

☐ Implies aspect was not addressed

▨ Implies aspect was addressed

■ Implies aspect was addressed in details

2.4   The Research Problem

Numerous IT and SOA governance frameworks have been proposed. However, there are no guidelines to adopt these frameworks and no evidence regarding their implications and their success rate. What emerges as a critical issue in any adoption of SOA governance is not which governance framework to choose, but more importantly to identify and focus on SOA particular aspects that need to be addressed irrespective of the framework. This research therefore first examines a range of aspects of SOA governance that are of key importance when an organization adopts an IT or SOA governance framework, and then validates these aspects in the real world of SOA. What are the key business and technical aspects of SOA governance that are critical for its effective implementation remains an important research problem.

On the other side, there have been many SOA governance frameworks proposed. Most of them are based on theories and they do not provide guidelines on how to be applied by the organizations. There is a need to have a conceptual list of aspects to be used to assess the effectiveness of SOA governance practices [12, 13, 16, 28, 39]. As it is unclear what organizations are doing in practice, what is needed beyond the current research is a study of the real-world adoption of SOA across the enterprise and the aspects of SOA governance that aid such adoption. This is critical for a better understanding of this popular architectural concept that is being rapidly adopted by industry organizations [2]. Studies of the aspects of SOA governance are crucial as the number of SOA implementations grows. Therefore, we need to know if IT and SOA governance efforts are well integrated with overall corporate governance arrangements in the organization; and how effective are IT and SOA governance arrangements within the organization [25, 40–42]. This proposed research could well provide executives with some guidelines on how to practice effective governance (directing and controlling of IT resources).

2.5   Research Aims

The paper aims to contribute to knowledge about effective implementation of SOA governance in organizations that adopt either IT or SOA governance frameworks. It provides a conceptual list of aspects – to be verified in practice – that contribute to effective SOA governance. As a result the research will make the following contribution to literature and practice. The contribution to literature will consist of the list of aspects used to assess the effectiveness of SOA governance practices in selected organizations. The focus will be on the assessment of the importance of these aspects as listed in Table 1 and the identification of new aspects that have not been considered. Practically, this research will find out what organizations are doing in practice to address SOA governance, it will investigate whether and how IT or SOA governance frameworks are used and will also provide insights into the ways these frameworks are being used by organizations in practice and what problems they face as a result. Moreover, the list of SOA governance aspects will provide guidance for organizations to improve SOA governance.

3   Problems, Research Approach, Methodology and Design

3.1   Problem Statement

We can conclude that frameworks have been created but most of them address the technical aspects, others were satisfied with the abstract design guidelines and some others focus on specific management aspects [3]. We don't know to which degree SOA governance frameworks and processes have been adopted; there is also a gap in the literature related to the experience in using SOA governance frameworks and processes and how these models are related to SOA adoption. Therefore, the problem to be addressed in this research paper is that of assessing the level of adoption of SOA governance frameworks and processes in practice and to identify correlations between the level of adoption of SOA governance framework and that of SOA in general.

3.2   Methodologies and Design

Since the research problem statement is concerned with determining a common understanding of what SOA governance means in practice by highlighting the aspects of SOA governance frameworks, and since the number of organizations that have adopted SOA governance framework is likely to be small, this research uses an interpretive qualitative research methodology based on interviews as a first phase and in-depth field-study in the second phase, to address the research problem. Following a long tradition in qualitative, interpretive research in IS, Goldkuhl [43] claims that scientific knowledge should be based on the meanings and knowledge of the studied actors and also co-constructed through inter-subjective meaning by the actors and researchers making during the empirical study. Given that the focus of this study is the practice of SOA governance in real-life contexts and that the aim is to find out whether and how different SOA and IT governance frameworks are applied in practice so as to create an understanding of the discrepancy between theory (how frameworks should be applied) and the practice, an interpretive methodology is adopted involving a particular research design, discussed next.

Phase I – Interviewing Experts – An Interpretive Study

The first phase involves conducting interviews with experts who have experience with SOA governance in multiple companies and who participated in several SOA projects. The role of the interviews is to acquire a broad view of SOA governance issues at the time the study is done. The interviews will focus on the aspects of the governance frameworks used in practice. The expected outcomes of these interviews are the verification of relevant aspects of SOA governance found in the literature (as presented in Table 1) and the identification of new elements. The interviewees will be selected and recruited through professional networks of SOA/IT governance experts. The interviews will take the form of face-to-face personal interviews.

Phase II - In-Depth Field Study

The second phase – a field research study – will consist of an in-depth study of two organizations. One that has been highly successful with SOA governance and another one that attempted and failed to implement SOA governance. The selection of two cases will enable the identification and analysis of SOA governance aspects present in both, and those present in one of them. By contrasting SOA governance effectiveness in the two cases and the ways individual aspects are implemented will provide grounding for the development of substantive theoretical claims regarding the importance and role of SOA governance aspects. The aim is not to generalize empirically but to generalize conceptually and provide an account of SOA governance aspects. This phase will allow having direct, in-depth contact with organizational participants, particularly through interviews and direct observations of activities. Data collection in this phase relies on observing, listening to members, taking notes, getting involved sometimes, and running field interviews.

3.3   Data Analysis

Data analysis will be conducted during and after each phase. The interview transcripts in Phase I will be analyzed using Thematic analysis [44]. The empirical material collected in Phase II – including filed notes, interviews, and various documents – will be analyzed during the field work thus enabling raising new questions and directing the study towards interesting emerging aspects. Analysis of texts in both phases will proceed following Thematic analysis by first coding interesting ideas, topics, and concepts and then organizing them into themes and identifying links among them. Coding in Thematic analysis helps the researcher to build a systematic account of what has been observed and recorded [44]. The thematic analysis will proceed in three steps: The first step of data analysis will involve coding and categorizing the textual data often called an open coding. The codes will be described and all related texts compared and analyzed. As the codes take shape, looking for relationships between these codes comes next. This is called axial coding. Axial coding allows certain codes to be subsumed under broader headings and some abstract codes to be seen more crucial than others. The last step is called theoretical coding (or selective coding). It will involve the identification of the core category around the analysis focuses. It will ideally identify the core code or codes allowing a central story to be developed. Theoretical coding usually occurs later when major themes emerge; the core categories will be verified and revised after checking the data [44].

4   Preliminary Findings

4.1   Participants

This study is still at infancy stage. Three face-to-face interviews were conducted as part of Phase I. The interviewees are selected and recruited through professional networks of SOA/IT governance experts. Contacts were made in advance by email and one page summary of the research was sent upon request. Each interview was given one-hour. The interview questions were not given in advance. The participants had a decision-making role in their organizations and their experience with SOA governance varies from 7 to 25 years. They have worked with a minimum of two organizations and on different SOA projects at different sectors: telecommunication, government, information systems, IT Architecture, IT management, software services and software products. The participants have occupied the roles of Systems Analyst, Project Manager, Technical Architect, Enterprise Architect, and others. Table 2 summarizes the organizations profile and interviewees' roles at their organizations.

Table 2. A snapshot of the organizations interviewed

Firm	Industry sector	Interviewee
1	Software services	Project Manager
2	Government sector	Enterprise Architect
3	Software products	Systems Analyst

4.2 Results

A broad set of questions were asked regarding the participants' background, their experience with IT and SOA governance, the mechanisms used to select a governance framework, the benefits realized from selecting that framework, the aspects considered in the framework, how the aspects were observed, and the lessons learned.

The interviews demonstrate the need to assess and validate the governance aspects. During the interviews, the participants were asked to assess each of the aspects listed in the literature review and to evaluate its importance: Not Very Important, Important and Very Important (Table 3). The interview transcripts were analyzed using Thematic Analysis as mentioned in Sect. 3.3. First, interesting ideas, topics, and concepts were coded, and then organizing and grouping the coded concepts into themes and broader categories and identifying links among them. Finally, the themes were reviewed to identify similar patterns across the data from the three organizations interviewed. All participants have used different SOA governance frameworks at the organizations they have worked. None of them have used an IT governance framework for an SOA project. The participants' view to SOA was based on their own experience. They all agreed that SOA needs a governance framework, but more importantly was their view to the aspects to consider in the governance framework. They selected their governance frameworks based on their organizations' needs. They either modified the framework selected to match with their organizational requirements or built their own one.

As a preliminary analysis based on the three interviews, the most important aspects were: organizational changes, Enterprise Service Bus, process monitoring and evaluation, and service security. This is not to ignore the service performance analysis and infrastructure capability. All three participants discussed in details the Enterprise Service Bus as being critical to their organization's SOA governance framework. One of the participants pointed to a new potential aspect - the interaction with web services - and suggested that it could be as a new aspect rather than being included under "Enterprise Service Bus". The three interviewees conducted were used to adjust the interview questions of Phase I in order to capture additional empirical data and try to achieve the aims of this research.

Table 3. * = Not Very Important, ** = Important, *** = Very Important

Business Aspects	Interview 1	Interview 2	Interview 3	Technical Aspects	Interview 1	Interview 2	Interview 3
SOA Vision	*	*	**	Enterprise Service Bus	***	***	***
SOA roadmap	*	*	*	Srv. performance analysis	**	**	***
Centre of Excellence	**	**	*	Policy management	*	*	*
SOA Maturity	*	*	*	Best Practices deployment	*	*	***
Service lifecycle mngt	*	**	**	SOA Gov. Technology	**	*	*
SOA Business cap.	*	*	*	Infrastructure capability	**	**	*
Governance processes	**	*	**	Process monitoring & eval.	***	***	***
Organizational changes	**	***	***	Service transparency control	*	*	**
Service Portfolio mngt	*	*	*	Service security	**	***	***
Open srv. market-place	*	**	***				

5 Conclusion and Future Work

Since the study is still under development and more interviews are to be conducted soon, it is probably too early to comment further on the results. From what has been done so far, we conclude that the literature covers enough about SOA governance and SOA governance frameworks theoretically but there is a gap about the usage of these frameworks by organizations and how the selection and implementation of a framework affects SOA adoption. This research is seeking to complete Phase I by conducting a total of twenty interviews. When Phase I is completed, two organizations will be selected for Phase II: one organization that has been highly successful with SOA governance and another one that attempted and failed to implement SOA governance. Comparing and contrasting the results of the two phases will provide grounding for the development of substantive theoretical claims regarding the importance and role of SOA governance aspects.

References

1. Luthria, H., Rabhi, F.: Service-oriented computing in practice – an agenda for research into the factors influencing the organizational adoption of service oriented architectures. J. Theor. Appl. Electron. Commer. Res. **4**(1), 39–56 (2009)
2. Beimborn, D., et al.: The role of IT/business alignment for achieving SOA business value - proposing a research model. In: Americas Conference on Information Systems (AMCIS). AIS Electronic Library (AISeL) (2009)
3. Müller, I., Han, J., Schneider, J.-G., Versteeg, S.: A conceptual framework for unified and comprehensive SOA management. In: Feuerlicht, G., Lamersdorf, W. (eds.) ICSOC 2008. LNCS, vol. 5472, pp. 28–40. Springer, Heidelberg (2009)

4. Varadan, R., et al.: Increasing business flexibility and SOA adoption through effective SOA governance. IBM Syst. J. **47**(3), 473–488 (2008)
5. Bernhardt, J., Seese, D.: A conceptual framework for the governance of service-oriented architectures. In: Feuerlicht, G., Lamersdorf, W. (eds.) ICSOC 2008. LNCS, vol. 5472, pp. 327–338. Springer, Heidelberg (2009)
6. Choi, J., Nazareth, D.L., Jain, H.K.: Implementing service-oriented architecture in organizations. J. Manage. Inf. Syst. **26**(4), 253–286 (2010)
7. Rabhi, F.A., et al.: A service-oriented architecture for financial business processes. Inf. Syst. eBus. Manage. **5**(2), 185–200 (2007)
8. SoftwareAG.: Best practices for SOA governance user survey. www.softwareag.com/Corporate/res/SOAGovernanceSurvey.asp (2008). Accessed 7 March 2011
9. Smith, F.O.: As SOA adoption solidifies, good governance is recognized as critical next step. Manuf. Bus. Technol. **26**(6), 48–49 (2008)
10. Parachuri, D., Badveeti, N., Mallick, S.: Light weight SOA governance a case study. In: IEEE Congress on Services - Part I (2008)
11. Lundquist, E.: The five next steps in service-oriented architectures. eWeek **26**(19), 22 (2009)
12. Niemann, M., et al.: Challenges of governance approaches for service-oriented architectures. In: 3rd IEEE International Conference on Digital Ecosystems and Technologies 2009, DEST '09 (2009)
13. Hassanzadeh, A., Namdarian, L., Elahi, Sb: Developing a framework for evaluating service oriented architecture governance (SOAG). Knowl.-Based Syst. **24**(5), 716–730 (2011)
14. High, J.R., Krishnan, G., Sanchez, M.: Creating and maintaining coherency in loosely coupled systems. IBM Syst. J. **47**(3), 357–376 (2008)
15. Laurent, W.: A better era of SOA governance. DM Rev. **18**(10), 29 (2008)
16. Larrivee, B.: SOA: no governance needed. Or is it? AIIM E-DOC **21**(5), 24–25 (2007)
17. Hojaji, F., Shirazi, M.R.A.: A comprehensive SOA governance framework based on COBIT. In: 2010 6th World Congress on Services (SERVICES-1) (2010)
18. Jordan, E., Musson, D.: Corporate governance and IT governance: exploring the board's perspective (2004)
19. ITGI.: Control Objectives for Information and Relates Technology (CoBIT) 4.1. IT Governance Institute (ITGI) (2007)
20. ITGI.: The Val IT Framework. IT Governance Institute (ITGI), Rolling Meadows, IL (2007)
21. Simonsson, M., Johnson, P., Ekstedt, M.: The effect of IT governance maturity on IT governance performance. Inf. Syst. Manage. **27**(1), 10–24 (2010)
22. The risk IT framework. ISACA 2009. www.isaca.org, 10 May 2011
23. COBIT 5 - A Business Framework For The Governance And Management of Enterprise IT. ISACA 2012, 26 Apr 2012
24. Weill, P., Ross, J.W.: How Top Performers Manage IT Decision Rights for Superior Results. Harvard Business School Press, Cambridge (2004)
25. Bieberstein, N., et al.: Service-Oriented Architecture (SOA) Compass: Business Value, Planning, and Enterprise Roadmap. IBM developerWorks Series, 1st edn., 272 pp. IBM Press, Indianapolis (2006)
26. Derler, P., Weinreich, R.: Models and tools for SOA governance. In: Draheim, D., Weber, G. (eds.) TEAA 2006. LNCS, vol. 4473, pp. 112–126. Springer, Heidelberg (2007)
27. Kuang-Yu, P., Shao-Chen, L., Ming-Tsung, C.: A study of design and implementation on SOA governance: a service oriented monitoring and alarming perspective. In: IEEE International Symposium on Service-Oriented System Engineering 2008, SOSE '08 (2008)

28. Niemann, M., et al.: Towards a generic governance model for service-oriented architectures. In: Americas Conference on Information Systems (AMCIS). AIS Electronic Library, Toronto (2008)

29. de Leusse, P., Dimitrakos, T., Brossard, D.: A governance model for SOA. In: IEEE International Conference on Web Services 2009. ICWS 2009 (2009)

30. Hojaji, F., Shirazi, M.R.A.: AUT SOA governance: a new SOA governance framework based on COBIT. In: 2010 3rd IEEE International Conference on Computer Science and Information Technology (ICCSIT) (2010)

31. Hojaji, F., Shirazi, M.R.A.: Developing a more comprehensive and expressive SOA governance framework. In: 2010 the 2nd IEEE International Conference on Information Management and Engineering (ICIME) (2010)

32. Afshar, M.: SOA governance: framework and best practices (2007). http://www.oracle. com/us/technologies/soa/oracle-soa-governance-best-practice-066427.pdf, 25 Apr 2011

33. WebMethods. SOA governance - enabling sustainable success with SOA (2006). http:// www1.webmethods.com/PDF/whitepapers/SOA_Governance.pdf, Oct 2006–March 2008

34. Woolf, B.: Introduction to SOA governance. developerWorks (2006). https://www.ibm. com/developerworks/library/ar-servgov/, 25 July 2010

35. Brown, W., Moore, G., Tegan, W.: SOA governance – IBM's approach (2006). ftp://ftp. software.ibm.com/software/soa/pdf/SOA_Gov_Process_Overview.pdf.   Aug   2006–July 2008

36. Holley, K., Palistrant, J., Graham, S.: Effective SOA governance. On demand business (2006). http://www-304.ibm.com/jct03001c/industries/global/files/educ_soa_gov_process_ overview.pdf

37. Zhang, Y., Xiang, G., Liu, W.: On airlines sustainable innovation driven by SOA governance. In: 2009 International Conference on Information Management, Innovation Management and Industrial Engineering (2009)

38. Poi, S., et al.: Enabling SOA through organizational change and governance - White paper, Nov 2007

39. Falkl, J., et al.: IBM advantage for SOA governance standards. http://download.boulder. ibm.com/ibmdl/pub/software/dw/webservices/ws-soagovernanceadv/ ws-soagovernanceadv-pdf.pdf, Aug 2009

40. Keen, M., et al.: Implementing Technology to Support SOA Governance and Management. IBM Redbooks, Indianapolis (2007)

41. Bieberstein, N., et al.: Impact of service-oriented architecture on enterprise systems, organizational structures, and individuals. IBM Syst. J. **44**(4), 691–708 (2005)

42. Josuttis, N.M.: SOA in Practice. O'Reilly, Sebastopol (2007)

43. Goldkuhl, G.: Pragmatism vs interpretivism in qualitative information systems research. Eur. J. Inf. Syst. **21**(2), 135–146 (2012)

44. Ezzy, D.: Qualitative Analysis: Practice and Innovation. Allen & Unwin, Crows Nest (2002)

Understanding a Transformation Process from Product-Centric to Customer-Centric Services in a Financial Institution - A Work System Perspective

Vijaya Murthy and Olivera Marjanovic[✉]

The University of Sydney Business School, Sydney, NSW 2006, Australia
{vijaya.murthy, olivera.marjanovic}@sydney.edu.au

Abstract. This research aims to contribute to building an increased understanding of the strategic, business, cultural as well as other changes in an organisation's transition process from product-centric to customer-centric services. This paper offers an exploratory case study conducted in a complex financial organisation in the context of their customer-facing services. The transition process is examined through a theoretical lens of the *Work System Theory (WST),* following the argument previously made by other researchers that service systems could be seen as work systems. This holistic theory enabled the researchers to capture the three key phases of the transition process as work systems snapshots and show the manner in which the transitions occurred from one phase to another. More importantly, WST enabled an in-depth study of the transition process through the complex and unfolding interplay of strategy, customers, products and services, processes, people, information and technology, tracing the key challenges and success factors.

Keywords: Customer-centric services · Financial services · Case study · Work System Theory · Qualitative research · Customer-centric transformation

1 Introduction

The service sector has grown over the last 50 years to dominate economic activity [1], no longer only in advanced economies, but in all economies [2]. Consequently, the global landscape of business and society is increasingly seen as a very large global service ecosystem [3]. While in the past the term *"service systems"* was predominantly associated with technology because of its system component, this is no longer the case. Service systems are now considered to be a complex and very dynamic configuration of people, technologies, organizations and shared information that create and deliver value to customers, providers and other stakeholders [3]. "The smallest service system centres on an individual as he or she interacts with others, and the largest service system comprises the global economy" [4, p. 18].

In spite of their growing importance, scientific understanding of modern services is still rudimentary [1]. Many academic disciplines, from technical to organisational and social sciences, have accumulated knowledge relevant to understanding a service

J.G. Davis et al. (Eds.): ASSRI 2013, LNBIP 177, pp. 29–43, 2014.
DOI: 10.1007/978-3-319-07950-9_3, © Springer International Publishing Switzerland 2014

system, but each remains focused on different aspects of the overall system [4]. Relevant research remains in unconnected academic and research silos [1]. Yet "research in service innovation requires cross-disciplinary work" [5].

The ever-increasing complexity of service systems calls for an integrated, multi-disciplinary approach. This in turn requires common foundations including shared concepts and theories. As a starting point we adopt the following definition of Services Sciences, as previously proposed by Bitner et al. [5]. "*Services Sciences is an emerging discipline that focuses on fundamental science, models, theories and applications to drive innovation, competition, and quality of life through services(s)*" [5, p. 228].

Furthermore, the so-called *service-dominant* logic (S-D logic) proposed by Vargo and Lusch's [2] is widely seen to provide "just the right perspective, vocabulary, and assumptions on which to build a theory of service systems, their configurations, and their mode of interaction" [4]. First developed in marketing, S-D logic is now widely considered to provide the philosophical foundations for service science, with the concept of "service system" being its basic theoretical construct. Service systems are seen as complex business and societal systems that create benefits for customers, providers, and other stakeholders [6]. More importantly, service systems engage in, and focus on knowledge-based interactions to co-create knowledge [4] and as such are expected to provide a more sustainable source of competitive advantage in the knowledge economy.

Services are no longer perceived just as add-ons to products or as after-thought of product delivery (e.g. after-sales customer care). S-D logic acknowledges the fact that in order to remain competitive many companies are now shifting from *Product-dominated logic (P-D logic),* to services and not only in manufacturing. However, any transition from products (P-D logic) to S-D logic is a very complex process.

This paper focuses on a transition process from *product-centric* to *customer-centric* services in a financial service company, aiming to contribute to building an increased understanding of the strategic, cultural as well as other changes experienced in the transition process. More precisely, this paper offers an exploratory case study conducted in a complex financial organisation in the context of their customer-facing services, examining the transition from their services structured around financial products to the new ones focused on customer. The transition process is examined through a theoretical lens of the *Work System Theory* (WST) [7–16] following the argument that service systems could be seen as work systems [7]. This holistic theory enabled us to capture the three key phases of the transition process as work systems snapshots and show the manner in which the transitions occurred from one phase to another.

This innovative approach provided the researchers an in-depth insight into key issues related to organisational environment, strategy, customers, products and services, processes & activities, participants, information and technologies – all relevant for each phase of the transition process. More importantly, WST enabled the researchers to study the transition process through the complex and unfolding inter-play of these elements, tracing the key aspects and its success factors.

The next section introduces the related work on the emerging field of service sciences research. This is followed by an introduction to the Work Systems Theory used as the theoretical lens for this research. After presenting the case organization and the research method, the paper proceeds to describe the main research findings. The final section describes conclusions, limitation and future work.

2 Related Work

Service-oriented thinking is one of the fastest growing paradigms in today's economy with relevance to many disciplines including information technology, information systems, accounting, finance, marketing, operations [17]. As stated, many research disciplines are already working on various aspects and perspectives of service systems. However, their efforts and research contributions still remain in unconnected research silos as "precious few attempts to integrate them have been undertaken" [1, p. 36]. This silo approach to service research has resulted in "conceptual confusion" [1, p. 36], best illustrated by numerous definitions of the fundamental concept of *service*, ranging from technical IT-enabled services on one end, to customer-centric business service on the other.

As the starting point in this research we adopt a definition proposed by Spohrer et al. [18] who define a service as *the application of competence and knowledge to create value between its providers and receivers*. This value is created from the interactions of service systems that involve people, technology, organisations, and shared information including language, laws, norms, shared models, measures etc. [18]. Furthermore, service systems are seen as complex business and societal systems that create benefits for customers, providers and other stakeholders [6].

Prior research confirms that effective competing through services require the entire organisation to view and approach both itself and the market with S-D logic [19] "It is a logic that is philosophically grounded in a commitment to collaborative processes with customers, partners and employees; a logic that challenges management at all levels to be of service to all the stakeholders;" [19, p. 5].

So far, companies focusing on service innovation are adopting two different approaches, as confirmed by Bitner and Brown [20]. The first one is to focus on making service more cost-effective through increased productivity and efficiency. The second, more complex approach is to focus on developing new services or improving the service experience. Regardless of the approach taken, companies are faced with an increasing push to compete on the basis of services [20].

However, while managers are aware of the links among services, competitive advantage and firm performance, they often fail to execute on that knowledge, in spite of being motivated to perform [21]. At the same time, "academics, though aware of these links, have not sufficiently informed normative theory to adequately assist in that execution" [19, p. 5]. This is the *first* research gap relevant for this project. To fill this gap, we use a formal theory to develop a better understanding of an organisation's adoption of services, motivated by its objective to attain a more sustainable source of competitive advantage.

Furthermore, prior literature also confirms a research gap related to the capabilities required to enact S-D logic or in other words transition from product orientation to service orientation. While the managerial aspects of different notions of value co-creation have been widely discussed in the literature, "managers only have limited guidance in the literature for implementing S-D practices" [22, p. 21]. The process of "servicialization" has been recognised as a research challenge [23, 24] and an answer is not found to date. As pointed out by Stauss [25], a service science that focuses on this process and its challenges has a clear and relevant focus. This is even more important "because the available research contributions highlight merely the industrial perspectives, with the focus on product, technology, efficiency and costs. Therefore, there is a risk of the traditional customer-oriented perspective of service research having to take back seat" [25, p. 67]. Recent literature confirms that the same research gap related to transition from product to service orientation still exists [26] and includes it in the service research priority list.

This is the *second* research gap we aim to address through our research, by focusing on identification and analysis of the key aspects of the transition process from product-centric services to customer-centric service in the case organisation. These key aspects are identified through an application of the Work Systems Theory, explained in the next section.

3 Foundation Theory

3.1 An Overview of Work System Theory

The Work System Theory (WST) by Alter [7–16] is a theory proposed to bridge the gap between research and practice, by helping business professionals attain a good understanding of a work system, how well it performs and how it might be improved [16, p. 3]. At the same time, "Academic researchers can apply it for gaining a deeper appreciation of past research and for developing future research projects" [16, p. 2]. Alter argues that in order to develop even a rudimentary understanding of a work system by empirical research it is necessary to acquire knowledge of the customers, products and services, processes and activities, participants, information, and technologies [11].

"A work system is a system in which human participants and/or machines perform work using information, technology and other resources to produce products and/or services for internal or external customers" [11, p. 451]. The examples include any project, supply-chain, e-commerce web site, loan approval [11, 13] and in more recent times, service systems [8], as elaborated in the next sub-section.

The work system framework (depicted by Fig. 1), "identifies nine elements that are part of even a rudimentary understanding of a work system". [11, p. 465]. The arrows represent the links through which a change in one element can affect the other elements. The framework provides a visual representation of a static view of a work system's form and function during a particular time period.

Overall, the work system framework provides "an outline for describing the system being studied, identifying problems and opportunities, describing possible changes and tracing how these changes might affect other parts of the work system" [11, p. 465]. Application of the work system framework to a particular situation is called a work system snapshot.

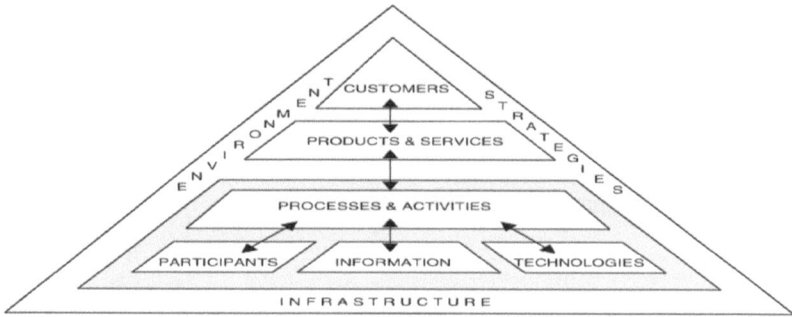

Fig. 1. The work system framework by Alter [11]

The main elements are briefly described as follows [9, 11]:

CUSTOMERS – the main purpose of any work system is to produce products and services for customers. Thus, customers (internal and external) are the recipients of a work system's outcomes.

PRODUCT AND SERVICES – they consist of information, physical things, and/or actions produced by a work system for the benefit or use of its customers.

PROCESSES AND ACTIVITIES – they occur within the work system to produce products and services. There must be at least one activity. Also, it is important to note that work being performed may not involve a set of clearly predefined and specified steps with their beginning, sequential flow, and end being well defined. Thus work systems could include activities and processes that rely heavily on human judgment and improvisation.

PARTICIPANTS - these are people who perform work within the work system, including both users and non-users of IT.

INFORMATION – All work systems use or create information that in this context is expressed as the so-called informational entities that are used, created, captured, stored, transmitted, deleted, manipulated, updated, and/or displayed by processes and activities. Examples include orders, invoices, job descriptions, medical histories, job offers etc. Informational entities could be of different granularity and could contain or be contained by other entities e.g. an order containing a line item.

TECHNOLOGY – this component includes both tools that are used by work system participants and automated agents performing automated activities.

ENVIRONMENT – this component includes the relevant organisational, cultural, competitive, technical, regulatory, and even democratic environment within which the work system operates and that affect its efficiency and effectiveness. Examples of organisational aspects include stakeholders, policies and procedures as well as organisational history, culture and politics.

INFRASTRUCTURE – This component includes the relevant human, information, and technical resources that are used by the work system but are shared by other work systems and managed outside of it. The infrastructure component is sub-divided into information infrastructure, technical infrastructure and human infrastructure.

STRATEGIES – The relevant strategies for each work system include enterprise strategy, organisational strategy and work system strategy. The work system strategy should support organisational and enterprise strategies and all three should be in alignment.

The Work System Theory and its central concept – work system – have been previously tested and adopted in numerous research and practical projects. For a very extensive list of these projects, see [10, p. 6].

3.2   Relevance of the Adopted Theory

As already indicated, the term "service" has been extensively used across different disciplines such as marketing, accounting, operations, computer science and infor-mation systems, but with very different and often inconsistent meanings and imple-mentation. In order to provide a unified view as well as a fundamental unit for understanding, analysing and designing services, Alter [11] proposes the term "*a service system*", following an argument that all services are delivered through service systems. Furthermore, he argues that "service systems are work systems" [11, p. 71]. "A service system is a work system that produces services for customers" [8, p. 202].

Viewing service systems as work systems means that the previously introduced work system framework and work system snapshot also apply to service systems and, as such, can be used as a basis of a flexible, business-oriented service analysis and design method. For example, the work system snapshots can be used to clarify the scope of an existing or proposed service and identify and describe the other work system components. They could be used to show the static view of how the chosen service system operates at a particular point of time. Most importantly, the work system perspective is applicable to all types of services. "The framework and the analysis and design approaches are applicable to a wide range of services: services for external customers and for internal customers; automated, IT-reliant, and non-auto-mated services; customised, semi-customised, and non-customised services; personal and impersonal services; repetitive and non-repetitive services; long-term and short-term services; and services with varying degrees of self-service responsibilities" [11, p. 72].

In addition to making service-related design choices more visible, the work system view of services facilitates an improved communication with business professionals, provides a common denominator for talking about services and provides synergy between different ways of looking at systems such as business, technical and func-tional (e.g. marketing, operational etc.). Most importantly, it emphasise the customer-centricity and as such further strengthen the core principle of service research and practice. Finally, Alter [11] argues that the work system view of services and service systems could be used to advance the current, multidisciplinary research of a science of service research that "could benefit substantially from an internally consistent and inclusive set of ideas that help in interpreting service research and practice" [11, p. 84].

Following the above-described arguments by Alter [8, 11], our research adopts the work system view and uses the associated concepts and frameworks to describe an organisation's transformation from products-centric to customer-centric services. The next section gives an overview of the case organisation selected for the research.

4   Case Organisation

The case organisation, a financial institution here named the NSW Bank (pseudonym) is one of the four leading banks in Australia employing tens of thousands of people. NSW bank has branches throughout the Pacific region and maintains offices in key financial centres around the world. The bank has global assets of few hundred billion dollars and ranks in the top 10 listed Australian companies by market capitalisation and has several million customers. The bank's operations comprise of five key business areas namely: Retail & Business Banking (RBB), Financial group (FG), Institutional Banking (IB), NZ Retail Bank (NZR) and Australasia Banking (AB). These five divisions are in direct contact with end-customers and were considered revenue generators.

These operations are supported by the back office (BO) called as Core Business Support (CBS). The BO operates the complete information technology division; supports and develops the software systems; provide infrastructure support for cash management, loan applications, fraud and anti-money laundering and security; and performs records management. The BO also develops, implements, and manages major projects and also controls the outsourced services by liaising with the outsourcing partners on behalf of the bank. The BO plays a pivotal role in developing the critical capabilities of the bank through strategic project execution and day-to-day delivery of core process outcomes.

After many years of focusing on competing through financial products, the NSW Bank adopted a new strategy focused on customer-centric services, because they believed that this would create a more sustainable competitive advantage. As a result, the organisation started transitioning from product-centric to customer-centric services. Hence, we chose this organisation for our study to gain an in-depth understanding of their transition process that remains an open research question as argued in the previous sections of this paper. The next section introduces the research method.

5   Research Method

In line with the exploratory nature of this research, a case study method that involved an interpretive approach was adopted as the most appropriate to capture and understand the contextual richness and complexity [27]. A case study is an empirical inquiry that investigates a contemporary phenomenon within its real life context when the boundaries between phenomenon being studied and context are not clearly evident [28]. Case study is an ideal methodology when a holistic, in-depth investigation is needed [29].

Prior research also recommends case study research as an appropriate method for service systems– in particular, their organisational aspects. "Case histories are a recommended method for understanding and adopting a service mind-set because doing so requires changing deeply held values, beliefs, and assumptions about the way things work. Changing employee reward systems may soon lead to new service-oriented behaviours, but it does not guarantee an authentic change in the deeper cultural mind-set that is truly sustainable" [26, p. 13].

As a case study this research could also be considered as a 'field research' since we as investigators immersed ourselves in the Bank to witness naturally occurring set of events and gain a firsthand knowledge of the situation [30]. We were 'outside researchers' or 'neutral observers' who carried out the study simply by collecting data and had no involvement in action in the field (NSW Bank) or in providing feedback to participants [31].

Since this is a case study, we designed our study to bring out the details by using multiple sources of evidence [27]. As per Hammersley [32] our 'case study' data is a collection of detailed, relatively unstructured information from a range of sources about the NSW Bank and includes the accounts of subjects themselves.

Hence we collected information from the NSW Bank's annual report, Sustainability Impact Reports, other internal documents such as their strategy reports, employee newsletters and external documents such as one-point contact commitment reports.

We also conducted interviews with 14 executives and 45 employees of the BO. The interviews started with a brief introduction for the purpose of the study and data required. The interviewees were assured of confidentiality and anonymity. The questions to executives were open-ended and revolved around the strategy of the bank; strategically important resources of the BO; challenges faced by the BO in implementing customer-centric services; and their individual role in development of important resources. The employees were asked to narrate stories on their work life experiences within the bank and how work gets done normally at the bank. We used stories to collect information from employees as we believed that story-telling could be useful for explaining strategy, managing change and engaging employees in contemporary organisations [33]. The stories enabled us to cover a broad topic area that allowed employees the freedom to choose any work experience they remembered. We observed that employees usually gave stories that focused on themselves, and described organisational activities that had a direct effect on them personally or their work. This process of story collection (both good and bad experiences) also stimulated stories around the manner in which the transition process affect an individual employee's work life. No lead questions were asked and the interviews were informal, building a rapport with the respondent. However, probing questions were asked during the process to access more information.

Informed by prior research that service systems could also be seen as work systems (Alter 2008), we focused our research on one service system called 'one point contact'. This was the main customer-facing service the NSW Bank introduced in order to implement its customer-centric service strategy. This core service will be explained in more detail in the finding section.

We performed data analysis by methodically identifying themes and building ideas guided by WST. By doing so, we were able to draw a picture of a fuller account of the connections between events and experiences. By combining data collected from interviews and the documents, we are able to offer an account of the Bank that transcends the individual voices of the participants [34].

We use the interpretive approach as we understand reality as holistic and socially constructed, rather than objectively determined [35]. Adopting such an approach for this study, offered us an opportunity to understand the happenings in NSW Bank through the meanings that people (in the Bank) assigned to them [36]. What we call our data are really our own constructions of other people's constructions of what they and their compatriots are up to [37, p. 9]. We as researchers are the measuring instruments and our understanding has been derived from our personal experience learned from theory rather than manipulating variables [38]. Thus, we have tried to grasp the 'meanings' of research participants' thinking and behaviour. By doing so we figured out that the transformation process of NSW Bank could be divided into three distinct phases that we captured by the corresponding WS snapshots. These phases will be elaborated in our findings section.

As a qualitative case study, our research involves a large number of documents and interview transcripts, which had to be managed, kept track of and coded methodically. Since we needed an efficient, consistent and systematic data management system, we opted to use NVivo software. All documents and transcripts were imported into the software which was later used for coding the documents according to themes as prescribed by WST. The use of NVivo software helped in making the study reliable and robust, enhancing transparency and the quality of the evidence could be judged [39].

6   Findings

6.1   Work System - Phase 1

The NSW bank's strategy was 'customer focused' and their 'mission' was to be number one for customer service in the banking industry. The bank aimed to deliver value across their business through the 'service-profit chain' and trusted that there was a direct link between superior customer service and sustainable profit growth. Therefore, in order to achieve superior service the bank intended to develop a 'high performance organisational culture' built around quality people, effective management processes and strong values. Based on their service-focused strategy the bank launched a new service system called 'one point contact' and decided to start focusing on the customer rather than products, which was the case before.

'One point contact' was a commitment from the bank to the customers that they would provide an appropriate answer (solution) within an appropriate time without passing the customers around. Also, the NSW Bank committed to consistently monitor their progress using a customer experience tracker survey and publish an external progress report on a regular basis. Thus, the bank believed that they could create long-term shareholder value by committing to provide superior services to their customers and adhering to it.

This had an effect on the way processes were conducted at the NSW bank that lead to two important changes. First, it was decided to provide training to the bank's employees (participants) to be able to deliver the 'one point contact' service system. Second, it was decided to automate their processes so as to enable participants to have immediate access to information about the customer in order to deliver 'one point contact' service system. Also, the bank decided to offer fully automated, customer self-service, available 24 h per day, 7 days per week, with an assumption that this would help improve the customer experience and increase loyalty to the bank.

Figure 2 depicts implementation process of one-point contact work system during phase 1. It illustrates the NSW bank's focus on two key elements – training the employees representing the Participants component of the work system (WS) (i.e. WS: Participants) to embrace high performance culture (WS: environment) and automation of service-oriented processes (WS: Processes, activities and technology). This was expected to result in improved employee productivity. The combined effect of high performance culture and improved productivity was expected to result in improved customer satisfaction and loyalty (WS: Customers) that over-time would translate into a more sustainable competitive advantage.

Fig. 2. Implementation of the "one-point contact" work system – phase 1

6.2   Work System - Phase 2

While the organisational strategy and the work system strategy were intended to be the same, in the second phase it became apparent that these two strategies were in direct conflict. The organisational strategy continued to focus on the big picture of customer satisfaction and high performance culture, but the work system strategy focused on a different objective i.e., cost cutting and economization, taking a short-term view.

Both these strategies were pulling the Bank in two different directions. This misalignment could be found in their process automation. For instance, when they had to decide and prioritize what to automate, based on the principles of the service oriented strategy, they preferred to automate processes that were expected to result in improved customer satisfaction. This could not be materialised since it involved large financial investments. Instead, they were compelled to automate processes that were focused on particular products because of cost pressures. Also, the bank was finding it difficult to transform the existing product-centric legacy infrastructure to a customer-centric oriented infrastructure, as systems and data had to be integrated across product silos.

Furthermore, they could not find the right mix of automation and human intervention that would enhance customer experience. This required the NSW Bank to shift from routine to knowledge work, yet they had problems in transitioning their employees from process to knowledge workers. To add to this problem, they were also not able to attract, engage with and retain a qualified knowledge workforce. They also had difficulty in shifting their employees' mindset from product to a customer-centric culture.

In this manner, the shift in the strategy on 'papers' resulted in disorientations within the Bank due to the contradicting nature of the strategies, which was also fueled by the prolonged time taken for the implementation of 'one point contact' service system. Contrary to the aspirations set by the organisational strategy, the end result was reduced competitiveness, as depicted by Fig. 3.

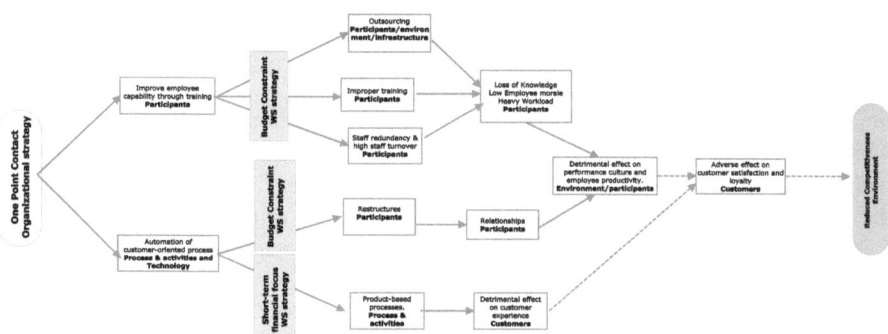

Fig. 3. Implementation of the "one-point contact" work system – phase 2

6.3   Work System - Phase 3

All the challenges identified in phase 2 were still present in phase 3. Figure 4 confirms that tension between organisational strategy and WS strategy still existed. The negative effects on employees (i.e. WS: participants) were the same as in Phase 2. However, in spite of the problems faced by NSW Bank due to the misalignment of organisational and work systems strategy, they started to move towards service orientation. The reason for this could be explained by the changes that occurred in three work system components, namely, environment (in particular, organisational culture), participants and customers. More precisely, the NSW Bank's initiatives to increase employees' awareness towards community volunteering started to gradually change the organisational culture. This turned out to be the key element which neither impacted on organisational strategy (of one-point contact) or the WS strategy (budget restriction). Employees were allowed to take one day off in a year to involve in community volunteering of their choice. The employees proceeded to involve in community volunteering in their own time (on weekends and after hours) still representing NSW Bank. The effect of this volunteering engagement was three-fold. First, the negative effects on employees created by the mismatch between

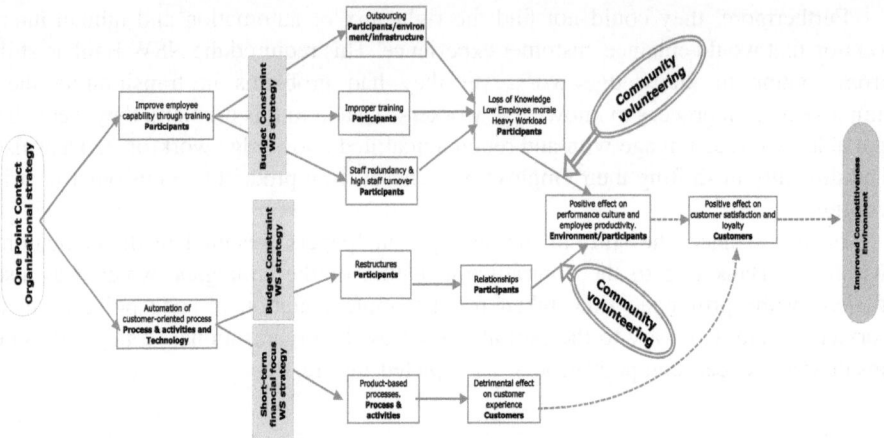

Fig. 4. Implementation of the "one-point contact" work system – phase 3

organisational and WS strategies were offset to a certain extent thus creating a positive work culture characterised by improved employee morale and commitment. Second, it had a positive effect on community in general. Employees' presence was noticed by the community and their (employees) contribution was valued and attributed to the Bank. Third, increased public visibility resulted in improving customers' impression of the Bank, thus having a positive impact on customer loyalty.

In summary, the Bank initiated the transition process from the organisational service oriented strategy of one-point contact, with an expectation of improved competitiveness. However, the way this transition process was implemented resulted in the opposite effect. The major shift towards customer-centric services was not initiated by the organisational strategy but could be traced back to employee volunteering (the WS Participants component). At the time of writing this article, the transition process was still in progress.

7   Conclusions and Future work

The main objective of this research was to contribute to the emerging multi-disciplinary research field of Service Sciences. In this context we used the Work System Theory to analyse strategic, cultural, and other relevant changes that occurred in the NSW Bank's transitioning process from product-centric to customer-centric services. Out research confirms the importance of mutual alignment between the organisational strategy and work system strategy, but also illustrates the complexities of this alignment. More precisely, we found that organisational strategy focused on the big picture and long-term vision of customer-centric service, but was implemented through the work system guided by the strategy still driven by the product-centric view of the business. This misalignment has slowed down the NSW Bank's transitioning process, as described in the previous section.

Furthermore, our research confirms the importance of organisational culture that needs to be understood in a broader context and beyond the service being studied. For example, in the NSW Bank the main impetus for the gradual change in organisational culture, necessary for the implementation of customer-centric services, came outside of the work system (i.e. service) being implemented. As it occurred parallel to WS implementation, not affecting its cost cutting and economisation strategy in any way, it could have gone unnoticed had we only focused on the service alone, without taking a broader perspective.

This case also confirms the previous observation that managers only have limited guidance in the literature for implementing service-oriented practices [22]. In the absence of such guidance organisations are left to their own experimentation. In the case of NSW Bank, the transitional process is confirmed to be complex and continuously evolving through experimentation and organisational learning. Most importantly unexpected and unintentional aspects of the process (community volunteering) turned out to be critical to the transition process rather than deliberate design and implementation of organisational strategy. The WST enabled us to take a holistic approach of a service system and through this capture this important aspect that could have been easily missed if we were to focus on implementation of organisational strategy, or just a single service being studied.

By definition, case study research is not generalisable [27, 28, 30]. Therefore, the outcomes of this research are not intended to be directly transferable to another organization. This is because every complex organisational environment is always unique. Even though the results cannot be generalised, we argue that the innovative approach of using the Work System Theory, in particular work system snapshots to understand the transition process from product-centric to customer-centric services is replicable in other contexts. This is the main research contribution of our work, as described in this paper. Our current and future work involves further study of the transition process from product-centric to customer-centric services in service industries through more case study research across different industry domains.

References

1. Chesbrough, H., Spohrer, J.: A research manifesto for services sciences. Commun. ACM **49**(7), 35–40 (2006)
2. Vargo, S.L., Lusch, F.L.: Service dominant logic: continuing the evolution. J. Acad. Market. Sci. **36**(1), 1–10 (2008)
3. IFM and IBM: Succeeding through service innovation: a service perspective for education, research, business and government. University of Cambridge Institute for Manufacturing, Cambridge, UK (2008). http://www.ifm.eng.cam.ac.uk/ssme
4. Maglio, P.S., Spohrer, J.: Fundamentals of service sciences. J. Acad. Market. Sci. **36**(1), 18–20 (2008)
5. Bitner, M.J., Brown, S., Goul, M., Urban, S.: Service science journey: foundations, progress, and challenges. ASU Center for Services Leadership
6. Spohrer, J.S., Demirkan, H., Krishna, V.: Service and science. In: Demirkan, H., et al. (eds.) The Science of Service Systems: Service Science: Research and Innovations in the Service Economy, pp 325–358. Springer, San Jose (2011)

7. Alter, S.: Work system theory: overview of core concepts, extensions, and challenges for the future. J. Assoc. Inf. Syst. **14**(2), 72–121 (2013). (Article 1)
8. Alter, S.: Viewing systems as services: a fresh approach in the IS field. Commun. Assoc. Inf. Syst. **26**, 195–224 (2010). (Article 11)
9. Alter, S.: Work system theory: an integrated, evolving body of assumptions, concepts, frameworks, and principles for analyzing and designing systems in organizations. In: Proceedings of JAIS Theory Development Workshop. Sprouts: Working Papers on IS, vol. 10, no. 80 (2010)
10. Alter, S.: Bridging the chasm between sociotechnical and technical views of systems in organisations. In: Proceedings of the ICIS 2010 Conference, St. Louis, Dec 2010, AIS. Paper 54 (2010)
11. Alter, S.: Defining information systems as work systems: implications for the IS field. Eur. J. Inf. Syst. **17**, 448–469 (2008)
12. Alter, S.: Work systems and IT artifacts: does the definition matter? Commun. Assoc. Inf. Syst. **17**, 299–313 (2006). (Article 14)
13. Alter, S.: A work system view of DSS in its forth decade. Decis. Support Syst. **38**, 319–327 (2004)
14. Alter, S.: The work system method for understanding information systems and information systems research. Commun. Assoc. Inf. Syst **9**, 23–39 (2002). (Article 6)
15. Alter, S.: A general, yet useful theory of information systems. In: Proceedings of the AMCIS 2000, AIS. Paper 22 (2000)
16. Alter, S.: A general yet useful theory of information systems. Commun. AIS **1**(13), 1–70 (1999)
17. Demirkan, H., Kauffman, R.J., Vayghan, J.A., Fill, H.-G., Karagiannis, D., Maglio, P.P.: Service-oriented technology and management: perspectives on research and practice for the coming decade. Electron. Commer. Res. Appl. **7**, 356–376 (2008)
18. Spohrer, J., Maglio, P.P., Biley, J., Gruhl, D.: Steps towards a science of service systems. IEEE Comput. **40**(1), 71–78 (2007)
19. Lusch, R.F., Vargo, S., O'Brien, M.: Competing through service: insights from service-dominant logic. J. Retail. **83**(1), 5–18 (2007)
20. Bitner, M.J., Brown, S.W.: The service imperative. Bus. Horiz. **51**, 39–46 (2008)
21. Bharadwaj, S.G., Varadarajan, R.P., Fahy, J.: Sustainable competitive advantage in service industries: a conceptual model and research propositions. J. Market. **57**, 83–99 (1993)
22. Karpen, I.O., Bove, L.L., Lukas, B.A.: Linking service-dominant logic and strategic business practice: a conceptual model of a service-dominant orientation. J. Serv. Res. **15**(1), 21–38 (2012)
23. Oliva, R., Kallenberg, R.: Managing the transaction from products to services. Int. J. Serv. Ind. Manag. **14**(2), 160–172 (2003)
24. Rust, R.T., Miu, C.: What academic research tells us about service. Commun. ACM **49**(7), 49–54 (2006)
25. Straus, B.: International service research – status Quo, developments, and consequences for the emerging services sciences. In: Straus, B., et al. (eds.) Service Sciences: Fundamentals, Challenges and Future Opportunities, pp. 57–70. Springer, Berlin (2008)
26. Ostrom, A.L., et al.: Moving forward and making a difference: research priorities for the science of service. J. Serv. Res. **42**(1), 1–33 (2010)
27. Yin, R.K.: Applications of Case Study Research. Sage Publications, Thousand Oaks, London (2003)
28. Yin, R.K.: Case Study Research: Design and Methods. Sage, Newbury Park (1994)
29. Feagin, J., Orum, A., Sjoberg, G. (eds.): A Case for Case Study. University of North Carolina Press, Chapel Hill (1991)

30. Singleton, R.A., Straits, B.C.: Approaches to Social Research, 4th edn. Oxford University Press, New York (2005)
31. Walsham, G.: Doing interpretive research. Eur. J. Inf. Syst. **15**, 320–330 (2006)
32. Hammersley, M.: The Dilemma of Qualitative Research: Herbert Blumer and the Chicago Tradition. Routledge, London (1989)
33. Cuganesan, S., Dumay, J.: Reflecting on the production of intellectual capital visualizations. Account. Audit. Account. J. **22**(8), 1161–1186 (2009)
34. Llewellyn, S.: Methodological themes: narratives in accounting and management research. Account. Audit. Account. J. **12**(2), 220–236 (1999)
35. Amaratunga, D., Baldry, D.: Case study methodology as a means of theory building: performance measurement in facilities management organisations. Work Study **50**(3), 95–105 (2001)
36. Deetz, S.: Describing differences in approaches to organization science: rethinking Burrell and Morgan and their legacy. Org. Sci. **7**(2), 191–207 (1996)
37. Geertz, C.: The Interpretation of Cultures. Basic Books, New York (1973)
38. Szmigin, I., Foxall, G.: Interpretive consumer research: how far have we come? Qual. Mark. Res. Int. J. **3**(4), 187–197 (2000)
39. Crowley, C., Harre, R., Tagg, C.: Qualitative research and computing: methodological issues and practices in using QSR NVivo and NUD*IST. Int. J. Soc. Res. Methodol. **5**(3), 193–197 (2002)

An Integrative Design Framework for New Service Development

Eng K. Chew(⊠)

Faculty of Engineering and IT, University of Technology, Sydney, Australia
eng.chew@uts.edu.au

Abstract. Service innovation is focused on customer value creation. At its core, customer-centric service innovation in an increasingly digital world is technology-enabled, human-centered, and process-oriented. This requires a cross-disciplinary, holistic approach to new service design and development (NSD). This paper proposes a new service strategy-aligned integrative design framework for NSD. It correlates the underlying theories and principles of disparate but interrelated aspects of service design thinking: service strategy, concept, design, experience and architecture into a coherent framework for NSD, consistent with the service brand value. Application of the framework to NSD is envisioned to be iterative and holistic, accentuated on continuous organizational and customer learning. The preliminary framework's efficacy is illustrated using a simplified telecom case example.

Keywords: Service concept · Service design · Service architecture · Customer experience · New service development · Service innovation

1 Introduction

With service science maturing and gaining wider acceptance by academics and practitioners alike, a growing interest in the theories and practices of service systems design and implementation [1, 2] has emerged, as exemplified by recent work on conceptual frameworks for guiding service systems design [3] and service networks innovation [4]. However, the observations that "the narrowness of much writing on service design" and "the dilemma of service design [as to] whether it is a product or a process that is being designed" have led Voss and Hsuan [5, p. 232] to argue for the need to *rethink service design* from a *cross-disciplinary* (including marketing, operations and information technology) *holistic* perspective, in the context of New Service Development (NSD) [6–8]. However, it remains a knowledge gap in the literature as to whether and how the disparate views of service design seen by marketing, operations and systems experts within a firm could logically be integrated to produce new *coherent* service designs. This paper contributes to closing this knowledge gap.

This paper pursues the research question: Could an integrative design framework be defined that would integrate the disparate business and technical views of service design into a coherent model that would ensure end-to-end design integrity? In particular, inspired by our initial informal dialogues with practitioners from large and new start-up enterprises concerning NSD challenges, the paper seeks to define a new

J.G. Davis et al. (Eds.): ASSRI 2013, LNBIP 177, pp. 44–58, 2014.
DOI: 10.1007/978-3-319-07950-9_4, © Springer International Publishing Switzerland 2014

integrative service design framework that will allow cross-disciplinary (marketing, operations and IT) experts in a firm to systematically co-conceptualize, co-design and co-implement new services, in line with the service strategy and brand value, to meet current or emergent customer needs, efficiently and effectively. We conduct an exploratory review of the extant literature and correlate, holistically and integratively, the underlying theories and principles of various disparate but interrelated *aspects of design thinking* for NSD, namely, service strategy [9, 11], service concept [9–12], service design [11–17], customer experience [16–21, 25], and service architecture [5, 26–30] which hitherto have often been analyzed individually in a somewhat fragmented manner. Using the basic principles and theories of service science, we correlate these different *aspects* of service design thinking and integrate them into a *coherent framework*. The efficacy of the framework is illustrated using a simplified telecom NSD case example [30].

The paper is organized as follows. Section 2 reviews the basic service science conceptual building blocks for constructing the proposed integrative service design framework. From the extant literature, the integrative design framework is then synthesized, in Sect. 3, design *aspect* by design *aspect*, with the *inter-aspect* relationships clearly articulated to ensure conceptual alignment and to minimize design conflicts or contradictions. Then, an exemplar telecom integrative design practice is described, in Sect. 4, to illustrate a preliminary operationalization of the framework. Finally, Sect. 5 concludes by summarizing the framework's benefits and limitations; and suggests areas for further study to reduce the limitations.

2 Conceptual Building Blocks

2.1 Process for Capabilities Integration

A service is defined as *a process* of applying the competencies and skills of a provider for the benefit of, and in conjunction with, the customer [31, 32]. A service offering is produced using the firm's resources including both tangible (such as goods) and intangible (such as knowledge, competence and relationship) assets [33]. The value characteristics of the service provisioned, however, are *co-created* through the interactions of the client's competences with that of the service provider [34]. Thus the client is *active* in a service interaction; it co-creates value (for itself) with the provider by *integrating* the provider's competences with its own [13, 34, 35]. Therefore, service is about "*the process* of parties doing things for and with each other, rather than trading units of output, tangible or intangible" [32]. Consequently, from the NSD perspective, service design is about designing the *processes* to facilitate resource or competence/capability integration by the customer.

A service firm (such as a telecom provider) is conceptualized as a service system [30] which is defined as a complex adaptive system of people, and technologies working together to create value for its constituents [36]. Thus, service innovation by a service system (firm) using NSD must be cross-disciplinary [5] and is only possible when the service system (firm) has information about *the capabilities and the needs of its clients*, its competitors and itself [37].

2.2   Value Co-creation in a Digital Ecosystem

In an increasingly digital world, information technologies are *"liquefying"* physical assets into *information* resources, and transform a service firm into a *value-creating* service system in which a *constellation of economic actors* (customers, suppliers, business partners and the like) are able to seamlessly *collaborate* to co-create value [38]. So the firm must establish *collaborative processes* with customers, partners, and employees to engage in the co-creation of value [39]. And the customer is regarded as an *operant resource* – a dynamic proactive resource that is capable of acting on other resources to create value for itself [32].

Value co-creation and innovation in the digital world would require firms to institute *individualized and immediate customer feedback* (to and from the customers) to engender customer and organizational *learning* [40]. This requires a *new* IT-enabled *organizational logic* which encompasses modular (multi-sourcing) flexibility, front-line (customer learning) focus, IT-enabled individualization and "connect and develop" innovation practices [40, 41]. In addition, the firm needs *new cooperation structures* by partaking in global competence clusters and practicing coopetition [40]. This means the service design framework must support selective participation by suppliers, partners and customers in the overall co-design process. And, customer experience design must incorporate customer learning and facilitate two-way feedback between client and provider.

Above all, to *be agile and adaptable* as they *learn of changing customer needs,* firms need to develop dynamic operant resources – the *dynamic capabilities* [42]. The dynamic capabilities allow firms to continually *align* their competences to create, build and maintain relationships *with* (thus the value propositions to) *customers* (the ultimate source of revenue) *and suppliers* (the source of resource inputs). Thus, the service design framework must institutes agile organizational and customer learning to sustain the service system's (firm's) dynamic capabilities and thus its evolutionary fitness.

2.3   Customer Centricity for Service Excellence

Customer is at the *heart* of value creation and service is about relationship with the customer [43]. The customer interacts with the service provider via the interface through which information/knowledge, emotions and civilities are exchanged to co-create value [34]. Value is wholly determined by the customer upon, and in the *context* of, service usage (and resultant customer experience), in which the competence of the provider is *integrated* with the competence of the customer to (perform 'a job' to) create (business) value with the customer [32, 43]. To win the service game, the value proposition must consistently meet the customer expectations and behavioral needs [20]. This can be assured by co-opting the customer competence in co-creating the service offering with the provider [44] – e.g. user toolkits for innovation [45]. However, the customer would collaborate with the provider in co-creation of core *service offerings* (in the context of service conceptualization and design practices) only *if* they would gain benefits, such as: expertise, control, physical capital, risk taking, psychic benefits, and economic benefits [19]. The service design framework must therefore support the potential for engaging customers in service offering co-conceptualization, service co-design and customer experience experimentation.

3 Proposed Integrative Service Design Framework

To create new innovative services that sustainably co-create superior customer value in the constantly evolving digital ecosystem, an integrated design framework is proposed. It is synthesized from the extant literature in accordance with the preceding conceptual building blocks. First and foremost, the proposed integrated design framework is founded on (Step 0 in Fig. 1) the firm's mission and service strategy focused on meeting the customers' existing and emerging needs. In particular, the firm's *brand value* and its subordinate service value proposition must resonate and align with the customers' requirements (or value expectations).

The integrative design framework for NSD (see Fig. 1) consists of *closely inter-related practices* of: (a) *service concept* which defines what the service is and how it satisfies customer needs [9–12], (b) *service design* which defines the service delivery mechanisms to consistently satisfy customer needs [13–17], (c) *customer experience* and value creation which guides service design *to align* the provider's competences and learning regime to those of the customers to ensure superior experience [16–25], and (d) *service architecture* which *systematizes* service concept, service design and innovation [5, 26–30]. These four interrelated practices and their underlying theories and principles are detailed below individually, but are typically practiced in the real-world *iteratively* and *holistically* – accentuated on agile organizational and customer learning for each and every iterative step such that the integrated design practice becomes the firm's dynamic capability enabling it to attain evolutionary fitness with the turbulent external market environment [42].

3.1 Service Strategy

Strategy (Step 0) is designed to fulfill the firm's vision and mission. There is a four-step approach to developing a successful service strategy: (1) Select the innovation

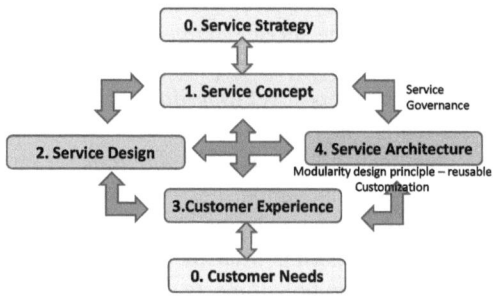

Fig. 1. An integrative service design framework

focus, such as new service innovation or service delivery innovation, and the target customer group(s); (2) Uncover customer needs in terms of jobs to get done and outcomes expected; (3) Prioritize customer needs; (4) Develop a service strategy (and attendant service concept) to fulfill the high priority customer needs [9]. A successful service strategy fits what the customer will value with what the company can deliver. This means aligning the *service concept* (what it would take to deliver on the customer value propositions), and hence the service architecture, with firm's capabilities, resources, culture and strategy.

3.2   Service Concept

A service concept (Step 1) defines the conceptual model of the service. It describes *what* the service is and *how* it satisfies *customer needs* [9]. Service concept is the most critical component of *service strategy*, and reflects the alignment of the customer needs (job and outcome opportunities) with the company capabilities. It reinforces the firm's brand strategy/value. Service concept also forms the fundamental requirements for *service design*, service development and service innovation [10]. It is developed as the *end-result* of the activities of strategic positioning, idea generation and concept development/refinement – a *marketing-led* cross-disciplinary endeavor. The conceptual model of a service consists of seven components which together define the *desired customer outcomes* (value propositions) of the service: service benefits, participation activities, emotional component, perception component, service process, physical environment, and people/employee [10]. To define an *innovative* service concept, Bettencourt [9] recommends that a service firm should: focus creative energies on specific job and outcome opportunities; identify where the key problems lie in satisfying high-opportunity jobs and outcomes; systematically consider a diverse set of new service ideas to satisfy the opportunities; and build a *detailed concept* with service *strategy* and service *delivery* in mind.

Service concept is the principal driver of *service design decisions* at all levels of planning and implementation. It relates to *service architecture* or service blueprint which guides service design, and to *service governance* which defines the decision rights and the decision making process for service design, planning and implementation [11]. For example, at the strategic planning level (*marketing-led*), the service concept drives design decision for new or redesigned services. At the operational level (*IT/operations-led*) it defines how the service delivery system implements the service strategy and how to determine appropriate performance measures for evaluating service design. At the service recovery level (*operations-led*), it defines how to design and enhance service encounter interactions. Thus service concept along with the overarching service architecture is the *common foundation* for new service development, service design and service innovation. For instance, service concept development and testing is at the *heart of service design* in new service development. Central to service conceptualization is declaring what the *customer value proposition* is in relation to the firm's *strategic intent*, how it meets the customer needs and what is the service logic required in delivering the value proposition [11]. Service concept articulates the service operation – why and how the service is delivered (in line with the brand value); the service experience – i.e. customer experience; the service out-come – i.e. customer benefits; and the service value – i.e. the perceived customer benefits minus the service cost [12]. Service concept and the corresponding service design (described below) are intended to *reflect the service firm's business strategy* and brand value, and therefore directly impact the firm's financial performance.

3.3 Service Design

Service design (Step 2) – an *IT/operations-led* cross-disciplinary endeavor – starts with the customer/user and defines how the service will be performed using human-centered and user-participatory methods to model the service performance [15].

We distinguish service design at two levels: new service development (NSD) at the individual service offering level (akin to new product development in manufac-turing), and service system at the service firm level (akin to enterprise design).

From NSD perspective, a service is conceptualized as an open system with cus-tomers being present everywhere. Service design must address strategic service issues such as marketing positioning and the preferred type of customer relationship, in line with the strategic intent of the service organization. Service governance is also required to monitor the service qualities and financial performance against the design outputs. The framework for designing the *service delivery system* must address multiple interrelated factors: standardization; transaction volume per time period; locus of profit control; types of operating personnel; types of customer contacts; quality control; orientation of facilities; and motivational characteristics of manage-ment and operating personnel [11]. The service delivery system fulfills the firm's strategic service vision and is designed/specified by means of service blueprinting [16, 18]. Service blueprinting is a map or flowchart of all the transactions constituting the service delivery process. The map identifies: *the* potential *'fail-points'*; *the* line of interaction between client and provider known as *service encounters*; *the line of visibility* – above it employees actions are visible to the customer (directly affecting customer experience); below it is the 'back-stage'; and *the* internal line of interactions below the line of visibility [16, 18]. The *service encounter* design is a critical element of service design, because from the customer's viewpoint "*these encounters ARE the service*" [16]. The design focuses on maximizing the quality of 'service experience' by the customer. However, service experience is the result of the combined efforts of the 'back stage' information and processes and the 'front stage' customer handling – both must work *seamlessly in unison* in satisfying the customer request [17].

Taking an end-to-end view of service process allows designers to analyze the stakeholders' requirements, pain points and performance metrics from which service design (or redesign for an existing service) could be developed in collaboration with the stakeholders (including suppliers and partners) incorporating a combination of changes across process, organization, technology, and tool in an integrative manner [14].

NSD service design must include strategies for handling service variability to ensure sustained level of service quality expected by customers [17]. For instance, to manage an unexpected deviation from normal service encounter, the service design (per service strategy and governance) may incorporate the notion of service personnel *'empowerment'* which grants them the *discretion to recover* from service deviation (failure) by offering 'compensations' or alternative solutions to the customer to minimize adverse impacts to the customer [38]. Moreover, where multichannel services are provided, the design must ensure *consistent* service experience across all channels. Finally, service design needs to incorporate the requirements of *lean consumption* by the customers [21] (in accordance with the customer experience design principles described in the next section) and achieve the objectives of *service profit chain* [46].

At the service firm level, service design is concerned designing the service system (which offers the service) – akin to enterprise or organization design – to achieve the firm's mission and strategy, a C-level executive-led cross-disciplinary endeavor. Service system design must address the roles of people, technology, shared information, as well as the role of customer input in production processes and the application of competences to benefit others. Consequently, it will influence the design of service delivery system for each service offering created by NSD. This design interrelationship will be managed through the modularity principles of the attendant *service architecture* (see later). The design must also address the service systems' requirements for agility and adaptability in alignment with their environments [36]. A *learning framework* is necessary to sustain the firm's creative design ability, and improve and scale the service systems. The framework is designed to achieve three critical requirements: *effectiveness* – the *right things* get done; *efficiency* – things are done in the *right way*; *sustainability* – the *right relationships* exist with other service systems to ensure the system's long term sustainability [36, 37]. Sustainability is achieved through the service system's (brand) *reputation*, because excellent reputations naturally attract value propositions from other service systems wanting to co-create value. It also requires appropriate amount of *shared information* to be available to all service systems (the principle of information symmetry) to enhance coordination and mutual sustainability within the service ecosystem. The design is however inherently challenged by the *people factor*, as people are complex and adaptive.

In sum, service system design, broadly, must address *four* variables: *physical setting*; *process design* – the service blueprinting or mapping which designs 'quality' into the service delivery system; *job design* – the social technical job design which include addressing the employee motivational requirements; and *people* – the staff (competence) selection [11].

3.4   Customer Experience

Service design excellence strives to achieve superior customer experience (Step 3), where the design practice is focused on the usability and pleasurability of the service interactions [25, p. 84]. Service organizations are increasingly managing customer experiences to promote differentiation and customer loyalty. Due to its strategic significance as a competitive differentiator, this specialist design practice, whilst being an integral part of service design, is factored out as a crucial step deserving special attention in the overall design framework. Customer experience requirements of each service type are usually analyzed using use-case scenarios similar to that of service blueprint [16, 22].

Customer experience is influenced by the *service intensity*, which is defined in terms of the number of actions (frequency and sequence) initiated by the service provider, or the amount (and importance) of *information exchanged* in a service encounter or the duration of the service encounter [17, 25]. The service design of multi-interface system must unify service management, human computer interface, and software engineering perspectives into an integrated design embodying the customer experience requirements [22]. The experience-centric service providers design the *activity and context* of the experience to engage customers in a personal, memorable way.

Customer experience is contingent on the efficacy of service encounter design, which in turn is guided by the possible relationships between the *three parties* in the service encounter: the *service organization* (whether to pursue a service strategy of efficiency (cost leadership) or effective (customer satisfaction) or both); the *contact personnel* (following strict rules/order or empowered with autonomy and discretion); and the interaction between contact personnel and the *customer* (balancing conflicting "perceived control" by both parties) [13]. Technology could be designed to assist, facilitate, mediate or generate the service encounter, each with a different customer role in the service delivery process [13, 47]. Technology design therefore must account for potential customer (as well as employee) reaction so as to avoid future problems of acceptance [18].

The customer experience design must also address the complete "customer journey" (from presale, purchase, usage to expiry) and the attendant *dynamic engagement process* with the service firm [50]. The engagement can be emotional, physical, intellectual, or even spiritual, depending on the level of customer participation and the connection with the environment [23]. The experience is influenced by the effectiveness of value co-creation between the provider and beneficiary – measured by a composite of benefits (utility) and burdens (costs) [18]. Burdens relate to the service's usability or the degree of customer efficiency in 'consuming' the service [21, 48]. Thus, the most compelling service with the best "value for money" to the client is one that has the largest "benefit-to-costs" ratio. Service firms must therefore "consider not only the employees' productivity but also the 'productivity' and experience of *the customer.*" [18–21] From a service system viewpoint, customer value, created as a result of integrating the provider's resources with the client's, increases the client system's adaptability and survivability to fit with its changing environment [49].

Customer value creation process is a dynamic, interactive, non-linear and often unconscious process [24]. It is culminated from the customer's *cognitions, emotions and behavior* during the relationship with the provider, across the entire customer journey [50]. Value co-creation is determined in the context of the customer's *resource (and capability) integration* practice. To achieve optimal value, the *customer* processes, the *supplier* processes and the interfacing service *encounter* processes must *all* be aligned [24]. The process design must be congruent with the overall service architecture (see next section) to ensure consistent experience across all services and all channels (and devices).

3.5 Service Architecture

Service architecture is conceptualized to systematize service design and innovation. Leveraging concepts from product architecture, service architecture aims to create a common language across different views on service design and a systematic way to operationalize and measure the degree of service architecture modularity [26]. For a new start-up service firm, service architecture practice is likely to be non-existent (or immature). Service architecture capability emerges as the firm becomes more stable financially and growth is accelerating. It culminates in becoming a dynamic organizational capability. For mature firms service architecture features centrally as a reference framework for design governance (to assure customer-effectiveness and efficiency of all new services).

Service architecture is constituted in accordance with the principle of *modularity*, which in turn is characterized by five dimensions: *components* and systems as the basic modular units, the *interfaces*, *degree of coupling*, and *commonality sharing* between components, and *platform* as the overarching configuration of components and interfaces that make up the service architecture [27]. Modularity refers to the degrees by which interfaces between components are standardized and specified to allow for greater reusability and sharing of (common) components among service families. It provides the basis for mixing and matching of components to meet the mass-customization requirements; yields economies of scale and scope, and can help structure services to facilitate outsourcing. Platform strategies are the vehicles for realization of mass customization [27]. As platform decisions often cut across several service lines or divisional boundaries, platform strategic decisions must belong in the top management team who need to and can resolve cross-functional conflicts to jointly-achieve the firm overall strategy.

An important and challenging aspect of service architecture is the interface. Interfaces in services can include *people, information, and rules governing the flow of information*. Service interface can also include the flow of people. In general, an active role in service customization would be played by both the front-end employees and the customers themselves. This would suggest the service components need to be more loosely coupled than product components [28].

A service system can be analyzed, for the purposes of service architecture, in terms of four levels of increasing details in specification: industry level, service company/supply chain level, service bundle level, and service package/component level [26]. At level 0, the industry architectural template defines the value creation and the division of labor as well as value appropriation and the division of surplus or revenue among the different players. (This is the financial or commercial view of service design that is seen from the Chief Executive Officer/Chief Financial Officer level.) At level 1, the service company and its supply chain(s) are modeled both upstream and downstream. Both shared (internal cross-functional) and outsourcing of service components are important consideration for the service company level for economic and resource flexibility reasons, in line with its business strategy. (This is the operations management view of service design that is seen from the Chief Operating Officer level.) At levels 2 and 3, the service concept and service design activities of service innovation practice are harmonized and integrated to assure service agility. (This is the Chief Marketing Officer and Chief Information Officer view of detailed service design, operational and management levels.) At level 2, the individual service bundles of the service offering at the company level are analyzed – each bundle is viewed as a set of modules of service delivery, comprising the front- and back-office functions (and associated capabilities). The front-office design must comply with the above-mentioned customer-provider service encounter process design principles to ensure superior customer experience and optimal value creation (see Sect. 3.4 Customer Experience). At level 3, the service package and component level, the characteristics of the building blocks (components) are specified that con- tribute to the overall systems architecture, namely: standardization, uniqueness, degree of coupling and replicability [26]. Thus, service architecture enables *service agility* as new services can be designed and provisioned with minimal cost and little internal change, and the architecture can be dynamically adapted in response to external stimuli. But this would require support by a corresponding modular organi- zational architecture as well as IS architecture [26].

4   Exemplar Integrative Service Design Practices

Telecom companies (telcos), like banks, compete on customer service (experience) differentiation. Their missions, strategies and brand values are highly customer-centric which, through disciplined strategic alignment, strongly influences the ways their services are conceptualized, designed and operationalized.

A simplified telecom service system can be conceptualized as shown in Fig. 2. The telecom service system is composed of four service system entities (SSEs): the service provider SSE in collaboration with its IT supplier SSE and network supplier/ partner SSE delivers telecom service offerings to its customer SSE. The telecom service provider SSE consists of a collection of network- and systems-capabilities that together with the resources or capabilities of its partners and suppliers are configured (by service design) to create a differentiated service offering (composed of an

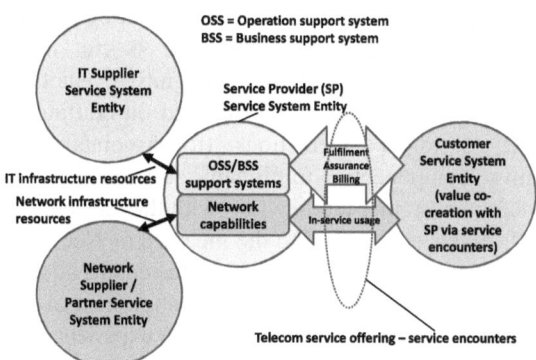

Fig. 2. A simplified telecom service system (Adapted from [30])

internally-standardized set of "service encounter" capability components/bundles: fulfillment, assurance, billing and in-service usage) for the customer SSE.

We illustrate below an *exemplar application* of the proposed integrative service design framework to telecom NSD based on this telecom service system model.

In *Step 0*, telecom business executive defines the competitive service strategy, often founded on customer intimacy value discipline [51], which is purposefully designed to satisfy the emerging or unmet needs of the chosen (existing and new) customer segments.

In *Step 1*, the product (marketing) manager informed by deep customer insights envisions and defines a new *service concept* (supported by operations and IT) – e.g. education institutions' emerging need for a virtual classroom service (in support of an innovative remote education service). This new service would allow geographically separated students from anywhere to participate in a real-time lecture from their home or office, using any device over any network of their choice, while still experiencing the same level of intimate interpersonal interactivity as if they were co-located in the classroom. At the service concept level, the focus is on conceptual (functional) requirements for the utility, usability and pleasurability (including exception handling) of the proposed service concept.

In *Step 2 service design*, IT and network experts will design (supported by marketing and operations) the integrated network and systems solution that satisfies the service concept requirements. Using the service architecture (*Step 4*) as a reference framework to leverage service component reusability and ensure the solution's fitness with the telco's overall portfolio of services, the IT/network experts may design, on one hand, a quadruple-play service solution (for "*in-service usage*" – see Fig. 2), combining broadband, mobile, IPTV and multi-media contents in an integrated service delivery (by configuring the appropriate network capabilities in collaboration of network partners/suppliers – see Fig. 2); and, on the other hand, design the appropriate accompanying customer "service encounter" capability components of fulfillment, assurance and billing (by configuring the OSS/BSS systems capabilities – Fig. 2) ensuring end-to-end service integrity in line with the espoused customer service strategy (Step 0) and the attendant customer experience criteria (Step 4).

In *Step 3*, *customer experience* design is typically led by systems designers with human factors engineering expertise [52] who are skillful in designing service encounter interfaces to satisfy the customer's cognitive, emotive and behavioral requirements. Customer experience design is focused on crafting pleasurable (often technology-facilitated) customer interactions (touch-points) with the "service encounter" capability components: fulfillment, assurance, billing and usage throughout the end-to-end customer journey [50] with the telecom provider. Customer experience design effectiveness is linked to the measure of Net Promoter® Score and consequently to firm's financial performance [52]. This entails aligning the end-to-end service encounter processes [24, 50] as well as the alignment of service capabilities between the provider and the customers to enhance the experience and productivity of each customer in using the said service [18–21].

In *Step 4*, the firm-specific *service architecture* is used as a reference model for governing the overall aforementioned service design practices. Telecom service design depends critically on the designer's understanding of the provider's service process (the OSS/BSS systems and digital network capabilities – Fig. 2) to ensure effective value co-creation accompanied by excellent customer experience. To that end, the telecom industry has specified a standard framework of telecom service provider business processes, known as eTOM (enhanced Telecommunications Operations Map) [29]. The eTOM reference framework has been adopted as generic telecom *service architecture*, Fig. 3, and can be used to specify firm-specific service processes, and to source commercial-off-the-shelf standards-based OSS/BSS software systems to support and, where appropriate, automate the specified service processes (business operations such as fulfillment, assurance and billing) [30].

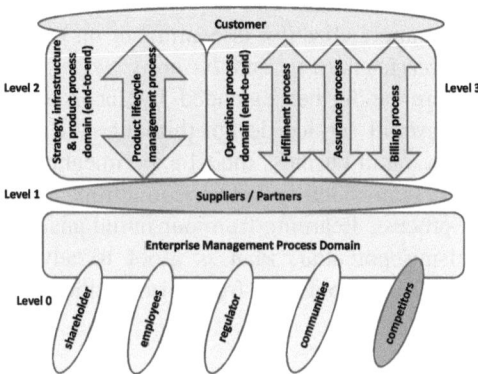

Fig. 3. Telecom service architecture (Adapted from [30])

5   Conclusions and Future Work

Service innovation is focused on creating customer value. Customer co-creates value with the provider by integrating their competences/capabilities with those of the provider. Thus customer productivity is as important as that of the provider in service provision as it impacts directly the service experience. At its core, customer-centric service innovation in an increasingly digital world is technology-enabled but more human-centered and process-oriented. This calls for research into whether and how cross-disciplinary holistic approach to service design would facilitate new service development and innovation.

This paper has used service science principles and theories to reexamine the different aspects of service design from the literature to explicate their logical and conceptual interrelationships. It results in a proposed new *integrative service design framework* which enables *systematic* joint service *conceptualization, design, architecture* and *innovation*, by cross-disciplinary experts from business, operations and IT. The strategy-aligned framework comprises four *closely interrelated practices* of: (a) *service concept* which defines what the service is and how it satisfies customer needs, (b) *service design* which defines the service delivery mechanisms to consistently satisfy customer needs, (c) *customer experience* and value creation which guides service design *to align* the provider's competences and learning regime to those of the customers to ensure superior experience and (d) *service architecture* which *systematizes* service concept, service design and innovation. These four interrelated practices are typically practiced in the real-world *iteratively* and *holistically* – accentuated on agile organizational and customer learning for each and every iterative step such that the integrated design practice becomes the firm's dynamic capability enabling it to attain evolutionary fitness with the turbulent external market environment.

The efficacy of the proposed integrative service design framework has been preliminarily validated by applying it to an exemplar telecom NSD in which telecom service environment is modeled as a service system. More case examples from diverse industries, however, need to be developed to fully validate the industry-wide applicability of the framework and to refine and improve its theoretical soundness.

Service innovation commercialization is contingent on careful alignment of the firm's *service strategy*, *service design* and *business model design*. The proposed framework could therefore be further extended by incorporating business model design principles in the overall service design thinking. We envision the enhanced framework would facilitate rapid business model experimentation of any new service concept to test its commercial viability before committing capital on the comprehensive detailed design process. Learning from our initial analysis of this conceptual extension shows promising potential. Plan is afoot to advance our preliminary knowledge of an integrative service design framework to the next level of theoretical and practical maturity.

References

1. Demirkan, H., Spohrer, J.C., Krishna, V.: Science of service systems. In: Demirkan, H., Spohrer, J.C., Krishna, V. (eds.) Service Science: Research and Innovations in the Service Economy. Springer, Boston (2011)
2. Demirkan, H., Spohrer, J.C., Krishna, V.: Service systems implementation. In: Demirkan, H., Spohrer, J.C., Krishna, V. (eds.) Service Science: Research and Innovations in the Service Economy. Springer, New York (2011)
3. Tan, Y.-H., Hofman, W., Gordijn, J., Hulstijn, J.A.: Framework for the design of service systems. In: Demirkan, H., Spohrer, J.C., Krishna, V. (eds.) Service Systems Implementation. Service Science: Research and Innovations in the Service Economy, pp. 51–74. Springer, New York (2011)
4. Agarwal, R., Selen, W.: An integrated view of service innovation. In: Demirkan, H., Spohrer, J.C., Krishna, V. (eds.) Service Systems Implementation. Service Science: Research and Innovations in the Service Economy, pp. 253–274. Springer, New York (2011)
5. Voss, C., Hsuan, J.: Service science: the opportunity to re-think what we know about service design. In: Demirkan, H., Spohrer, J.C., Krishna, V. (eds.) Science of Service Systems, Service Science: Research and Innovations in the Service Economy, pp. 231–244. Springer, Boston (2011)
6. Alam, I.: Removing the fuzziness from the fuzzy-end of service innovations through customer interactions. Ind. Mark. Manage. **35**(4), 468–480 (2006)
7. Edvardsson, B., Gustafsson, A., Enquist, B.: Success factors in new service development and value creation through services. In: Spath, D., Fahnrich, K.-P. (eds.) Advances in Services Innovations, pp. 166–183. Springer, Heidelberg (2007)

8. Edvardsson, B., Olsson, J.: Key concepts for new service development. Serv. Ind. J. **16**(2), 140–164 (1996)
9. Bettencourt, L.A.: Service Innovation: How to Go from Customer Needs to Breakthrough Services. McGraw-Hill, New York (2010)
10. Fynes, B., Lally, A.M.: Innovation in services: from service concepts to service experiences. In: Hefley, B., Murphy, W. (eds.) Service Science, Management and Engineering Education for the 21st Century, pp. 229–333. Springer, Heidelberg (2008)
11. Goldstein, S.M., Johnston, R., Duffy, J., Rao, J.: The service concept: the missing link in service design research? J. Oper. Manage. **20**(2), 121–134 (2002)
12. Clark, G., Johnston, R., Shulver, M.: Exploiting the service concept for service design and development. In: Fitzsimmons, J., Fitzsimmons, M. (eds.) New Service Design, pp. 71–91. Sage, Thousand Oaks (2000)
13. Fitzsimmons, J.A., Fitzsimmons, M.J.: Service Management: Operations, Strategy, Information Technology, 7th edn. McGraw-Hill Irwin, New York (2010)
14. Maglio, P.P., Srinivasan, S., Kreulen, J.T., Spohrer, J.: Service systems, service scientists, SSME and innovation. Commun. ACM **49**(7), 81–85 (2006)
15. Holmlid, S., Evenson, S.: Bringing service design to service sciences, management and engineering. In: Hefley, B., Murphy, W. (eds.) Service Science, Management and Engineering Education for the 21st Century, pp. 341–345. Springer, New York (2008)
16. Bitner, M.J., Ostrom, A.J., Morgan, F.N.: Service blueprinting: a practical technique for service innovation. Calif. Manag. Rev. **50**(3), 66–94 (2008)
17. Glushko, R.J., Tabas, L.: Designing service systems by bridging the ''front stage'' and ''back stage''. Inf. Syst. E-business Manage. **7**, 407–427 (2009)
18. Fitzsimmons, J.A., Fitzsimmons, M.J.: Service management: Operations, Strategy, Information Technology, 6th edn. McGraw-Hill Irwin, New York (2007)
19. Lusch, R.F., Vargo, S.L., O'Brien, M.: Competing through service: insights from service dominant logic. J. Retail. **83**, 5–18 (2007)
20. Schneider, B., Bowen, D.E.: Winning the service game. In: Maglio, P.P., Kieliszewski, C.A., Spohrer, J.C. (eds.) Handbook of Service Science, pp. 31–59. Springer, New York (2010)
21. Womack, J.P., Jones, D.T.: Lean consumption. Harvard Bus. Rev. **83**, 58–68 (2005)
22. Patricio, L., Fisk, R.P., Cunba, J.F.: Designing multi-interface service experiences: the service experience blueprint. J. Serv. Res. **10**, 318–334 (2008)
23. Zomerdijk, L.G., Voss, C.A.: Service design for experience-centric services. J. Serv. Res. **13**(1), 67–82 (2010)
24. Payne, A.F., Storbacka, K., Frow, P.: Managing the co-creation of value. J. Acad. Mark. Sci. **36**, 83–96 (2008)
25. Stickdorn, M., Schneider, J.: This is Service Design Thinking. BIS Publishers, The Netherlands (2010)
26. Voss, C.A., Hsuan, J.: Service architecture and modularity. Decis. Sci. **40**(3), 541–569 (2009)
27. Fixson, S.K.: Product architecture assessment: a tool to link product, process, and supply chain design decisions. J. Oper. Manage. **23**(3/4), 345–369 (2005)
28. Roth, A.V., Menor, L.J.: Insights into service operations management: a research agenda. Prod. Oper. Manage. **12**(2), 145–164 (2003)
29. TMF. Enhanced Telecom Operations Map (eTOM): The Business Process Framework, GB921, TeleManagement Forum Approved Version 4.0, March 2004
30. Chew, E.K.: Service science: a reflection from telecommunications service perspective. In: Maglio, P., Kieliszewski, C., Spohrer, J. (eds.) Handbook of Service Science, pp. 359–386. Springer, New York (2010)

31. Vargo, S.L., Lusch, R.F.: Evolving to a new dominant logic for marketing. J. Mark. **69**, 1–17 (2004)
32. Vargo, S.L., Lusch, R.F.: Service-dominant logic: continuing the evolution. J. Acad. Mark. Sci. **36**, 1–10 (2008)
33. Arnould, E.J.: Service-dominant logic and resource theory. J. Acad. Mark. Sci. **36**, 21–24 (2008)
34. Gallouj, F.: Innovation in the Service Economy: the New Wealth of Nations. Edward Elgar, Cheltenham (2002)
35. Gadrey, J., Gallouj, F.: Productivity, Innovation and Knowledge in Services: New Economic and Socio-Economic Approaches. Edward Elgar Publishing, Cheltenham (2002)
36. Spohrer, J., Maglio, P.P., Bailey, J., Gruhl, D.: Steps toward a science of service systems. IEEE Comput. **40**, 71–77 (2007)
37. Maglio, P.P., Vargo, S.L., Caswell, N., Spohrer, J.: The service system is the basic abstraction of service science. Inf. Syst. E-Business Manage. **7**(4), 395–406 (2009)
38. Normann, R., Ramirez, R.: From value chain to value constellation: designing interactive strategy. Harvard Bus. Rev. **71**, 65–77 (1993)
39. Lusch, R.F., Vargo, S.L., O'Brien, M.: Competing through service: insights from service dominant logic. J. Retail. **83**, 5–18 (2007)
40. Johannessen, J.A., Olsen, B.: The future of value creation and innovations: aspects of a theory of value creation and innovation in a global knowledge economy. Int. J. Inf. Manage. **30**, 502–511 (2010)
41. Chesbrough, H., Davies, A.: Advancing service innovations. In: Maglio, P.P., Kieliszewski, C.A., Spohrer, J.C. (eds.) Handbook of Service Science, pp. 579–601. Springer, New York (2010)
42. Teece, D.J.: Explicating dynamic capabilities: the nature and microfoundations of (sustainable) enterprise performance. Strateg. Manag. J. **28**, 1319–1350 (2007)
43. Edvardsson, B., Gustafsson, A.: J. Roos, I.: Service portraits in service research: a critical review. Int. J. Serv. Ind. Manage. **16**(1), 107–121 (2005)
44. Prahalad, C.K., Ramaswamy, V.: Co-opting customer competence. Harvard Bus. Rev. **78**(1), 79–87 (2000)
45. Von Hippel, E.: Perspective: user toolkits for innovation. J. Prod. Innov. Manage **18**, 247–257 (2001)
46. Heskett, J.L., Jones, T.O., Loveman, G.W., Sasser, W.E., Schlesinger, L.A.: Putting the service-profit chain to work. Harvard Bus. Rev. **86**, 118–129 (2008)
47. Froehle, C.M., Roth, A.: New measurement scales for evaluating perceptions of the technology-mediated customer service experience. J. Oper. Manage. **22**(1), 1–22 (2004)
48. Xue, M., Harker, P.T.: Customer efficiency: Concept and its impact on e-business management. J. Serv. Res. **4**(2), 253–267 (2002)
49. Vargo, S.L., Maglio, P.P., Akaka, M.A.: On value and value co-creation: a service systems and service logic perspective. Eur. Manag. J. **26**, 145–152 (2008)
50. Rawson, A., Duncan, E., Jones, C.: The truth about customer experience. Harvard Bus. Rev. **91**(9), 91–98 (2013)
51. Treacy, M., Wiersema, F.: The Discipline of Market Leaders. Perseus Books, Cambridge (1995)
52. Shaw, C.: The DNA of Customer Experience: How Emotions Drive Value. Palgrave Macmillan (2007)
53. Kaplan, R.S., Norton, D.P.: Strategy Maps. Harvard Business School Press, Boston (2004)
54. Anderson, J.C., Narus, J.A., van Rossum, W.: Customer value propositions in business markets. Harvard Bus. Rev. **84**(3), 91–99 (2006)

Smart CloudBench - Test Drive the Cloud Before You Buy

Mohan Baruwal Chhetri[✉], Sergei Chichin,
Quoc Bao Vo, and Ryszard Kowalczyk

Faculty of Information and Communication Technologies,
Swinburne University of Technology, Melbourne, VIC 3122, Australia
{mchhetri,schichin,bvo,rkowalczyk}@swin.edu.au

Abstract. In recent years there has been an exponential growth in the number of vendors offering Infrastructure-as-a-Service (IaaS), with a corresponding increase in the number of enterprises looking to migrate some, or all of their IT systems to the cloud. Prospective cloud consumers need to identify providers that offer resources with the most appropriate pricing and performance levels to match their specific business needs before making any migration decisions. However, no two vendors offer the same resource configurations, pricing models or provisioning models. Moreover, cloud vendors tend to use different virtualization techniques which impact the performance of the software systems running on top of their infrastructure. Since consumers only have a black-box view of the cloud, it makes the task of comparing and selecting appropriate computing resources a very complex exercise. In this paper, we present Smart CloudBench, which is a suite of software tools that allows prospective cloud consumers to *test drive* the cloud and *make purchasing decisions* based on price, specification AND performance. Cloud consumers can use Smart CloudBench for the automated, on-demand, real-time and customized benchmarking of cloud infrastructure and use the benchmarking results along with the pricing and specification information to make more informed purchasing decisions. Tests using Smart CloudBench show that the performance of higher priced servers is not necessarily better than that of lower priced ones, and it has to be tested extensively in order to substitute assumptions with facts.

Keywords: Cloud infrastructure selection · Performance benchmarking · Automated benchmarking

1 Introduction

In recent years there has been an exponential growth in the number of vendors offering Infrastructure-as-a-Service (IaaS), with a corresponding increase in the number of enterprises looking to migrate some, or all of their IT systems to the cloud. Prospective cloud consumers would like to obtain a quick assessment of the price, specification and performance of competing IaaS providers

J.G. Davis et al. (Eds.): ASSRI 2013, LNBIP 177, pp. 59–73, 2014.
DOI: 10.1007/978-3-319-07950-9_5, © Springer International Publishing Switzerland 2014

before making any migration decisions. While the pricing and specifications is public information, the performance of the computing infrastructure is unknown. Different providers use different virtualization techniques which impacts the performance of software systems running on top of their infrastructure; the only way to compare providers based on performance is benchmarking software systems on top of the cloud infrastructure and not relying on any assumptions based on price and specification. One approach to do this is to benchmark the cloud infrastructure performance by deploying own applications on selected cloud platforms and testing them under variable workloads. However, this approach can be complex, time-consuming and expensive, and very few organizations possess the time, resources and in-house expertise to do a thorough and proactive evaluation in this manner. A more practical alternative is to test representative applications[1] against representative workloads to estimate the performance of cloud providers. The benchmarking results can then be used to quantify application performance on the different IaaS platforms and to obtain valuable insights into the difference in performance across providers. By combining the benchmarking results with pricing information and resource specification, enterprises can better identify the most appropriate cloud providers and offerings based on their specific business needs.

In this paper, we present Smart CloudBench, a suite of software tools that allows prospective cloud consumers to test-drive public cloud infrastructure. It enables the measurement of infrastructure performance in an efficient, quick and cost-effective manner, through the automated execution and analysis of representative benchmarks on multiple IaaS clouds under customized workloads. Prospective cloud consumers can use Smart CloudBench to (i) select the representative application/s to use for evaluating cloud performance, (ii) configure the test harness, (iii) select and acquire instances on the cloud platforms to be tested, (iv) run the benchmark tests, and (v) aggregate the results to build a price/specification/performance matrix that can help with decision-making for provider and resource selection. The key benefits of using Smart CloudBench include:

- Reduction in time and effort involved in benchmarking cloud platforms. If the number of cloud instances to benchmark is high, and the number of representative applications is large, then manually executing the benchmarking process becomes a very cumbersome exercise.
- Reduction in performance testing costs. Since the cloud resources to be tested can be commissioned just in time and decommissioned immediately after completion of the tests, there are significant cost savings.
- Simplification of repetition of the benchmark process with reduction in human error.
- Automated and customized generation of reports and analytics for consumption by technical and non-technical audiences.

---

[1] Some example representative applications include TPC-W for a transactional e-commerce web application [5] and Media Streaming benchmark application for media streaming applications such as Netflix or Yuku [6].

– Centralised storage of performance data, which over time enables analysis of performance evolution.
– Performance benchmarking of cloud infrastructure can be offered as a service.

The rest of the paper is organized as follows: In Sect. 2, we briefly discuss performance benchmarking and how it relates to cloud infrastructure. In Sect. 3, we give an overview of Smart CloudBench and present its key components. In Sect. 4 we explain how Smart CloudBench works. We present some benchmarking results and discuss their significance in Sect. 5. We discuss related work in Sect. 6 and conclude the paper by discussing future work in Sect. 7.

2 Performance Benchmarking of Cloud Infrastructure

In the IaaS service model, the service provider gives consumers the capability to provision processing, storage, network and basic computing resources on demand. While the consumer has control over the operating system, assigned storage and the deployed applications, it has no control over the underlying cloud infrastructure. When a client requests and receives virtual machines from a cloud provider, it perceives the provisioned resource as a black-box whose run-time behaviour is unknown. The use of different virtualization techniques by different providers affects the performance of software systems running on top of the cloud infrastructure. Therefore, there is a need for tools and techniques to measure and compare the performance of computing resources offered by different cloud providers. Benchmarking is a traditional approach for verifying that the performance of a system meets the expected levels and to facilitate the informed procurement of computer systems. In the context of cloud infrastructure, performance benchmarking can serve a number of different purposes including (a) determining whether a particular server configuration meets the performance criteria, (b) comparing two configurations to find out which one performs better, and (c) determining the level of QoS that can be guaranteed to end-users of software systems deployed on the cloud infrastructure.

2.1 Elements of Benchmarking

The key elements of any benchmarking process are (a) *System Under Test (SUT)*, which refers to the system whose performance is being evaluated, (b) the *workload*, which refers to the operational load that is used to test the SUT, and (c) the *test agent (TA)* which is the test infrastructure that is used to carry out the benchmark tests. In our work, the SUT is the virtual cloud server whose performance we are interested in. It is viewed as a *black box*, whose operational details are not exposed and evaluation is based only on its output. The test agents are also deployed on cloud infrastructure as the cloud is perfectly suited to deliver scalable test tool environments which are necessary for the different types of performance testing. Thus, with Smart CloudBench, the cloud infrastructure forms the test environment and can also be used as the test harness.

There are two ways to benchmark the cloud infrastructure: micro benchmarking and application stack benchmarking. While a set of micro benchmarks can offer a good starting point in evaluating the performance of the basic components of the cloud infrastructure, application stack benchmarking offers a better understanding of how a real-world application will perform when run on top of the cloud infrastructure. Hence, we focus more on benchmarking the performance of the entire application stack. If prospective consumers can find representative benchmarks for their in-house applications, they can design experiments to match the internal load levels and load variations, and then test the representative application to determine how the different clouds compare performance wise and cost wise. By using representative performance benchmarking, consumers can quickly assess multiple cloud providers and their offerings in an objective, consistent and fully automated manner without having to deploy their own applications on the various cloud platforms.

2.2   Performance Characteristics

Performance is a key quality of service attribute that is important to both cloud consumers and cloud service providers. It should not only be specified and captured in Service Level Agreements (SLA) but should also be tested in order to substitute assumptions with hard facts. For example, intuitively, *a 16 GB server with 8 vCPUs is expected to perform better than a 8 GB server with only 4 vCPUs.* However, the actual performance benchmarking might reveal different results as shown in Sect. 5. In the context of cloud-based IT solutions and applications systems, the following performance characteristics can be of particular interest to prospective cloud consumers.

- *Time behaviour:* This performance characteristic captures the response time, the processing time and the throughput rate of the software system running on the cloud infrastructure, which subjected to a given workload.
- *Capacity:* This performance characteristic describes the maximum limits of the software system parameters i.e. the number of concurrent users of the system, the communication bandwidth, the throughput of the transactions etc.
- *Resource utilisation:* This performance characteristic describes the degree to which the amounts and types of resources are utilised by the system under a given workload. This characteristic can help identify over-provisioned and/or under-performing resources.

2.3   Types of Performance Tests

Depending upon the objectives of performance testing, there are different types of performance tests that can be carried out:

- *Response Performance Testing:* This form of performance testing is used to measure the responsiveness and duration of an IT system. This is conducted to understand the behaviour of the system under a specific expected load.

The load can be the expected concurrent number of users of the system performing a specific number of transactions within the set duration.

– *Stress Testing:* This form of testing is used to determine the boundaries of the SUT. A heavy load is generated to simulate unusual user behaviour and is used to determine if the system will perform sufficiently under extreme load conditions.
– *Soak Testing:* This form of testing is used to determine if the system can sustain continuous expected load without any major deterioration in performance. It involves testing the system with a significant load continuously over a significant period of time and observe the system behaviour under sustained use.
– *Scalability Load Test:* This test is used to determine how the SUT will scale for increasing load.
– *Spike Testing:* This form of testing is used to determine how the system behaves when subjected to sudden spikes in workload - will the system performance suffer, will it fail or will it successfully handle the dramatic changes to load.

3   Overview of Smart CloudBench

In this section we present a detailed description and reference architecture for Smart CloudBench. Smart CloudBench is a configurable, extensible and portable system for the automated performance benchmarking of cloud infrastructure using representative applications from a suite of benchmark applications. It also enables the comparison and ranking of different cloud service offerings based on user requirements in terms of infrastructure specifications, application performance, costs, security, geographic location, compliance, regulatory requirements and other requisite criteria [1,2]. It forms a key component of the larger Smart Cloud Broker suite[2] which comprises of the following additional components:

– *Smart CloudMonitor* - is a solution that enables the monitoring of cloud resource consumption patterns. It can be used in conjunction with Smart CloudBench to monitor cloud resource utilization during benchmarking in order to identify over-provisioned and under-performing configurations.
– *Smart CloudPurchaser* -enables the automated procurement and consumption of computing resources based on business rules specified by the cloud consumer [3,4].
– *Smart CloudMarketplace* - offers an open electronic market where multiple cloud consumers and providers can efficiently trade IaaS based on the supply and demand mechanisms.

The main components of Smart CloudBench include:

– *Benchmark Orchestrator (BO)* - This is the main module of Smart Cloud-Bench. It orchestrates the automated performance benchmarking of IaaS

---

[2] www.smartcloudbroker.com

clouds. It controls the entire process including benchmark and provider selection, workload description, resource management, workload generation, workload execution and result collection. It automates all the tasks that would be manually carried out in a normal benchmarking exercise.

- *Cloud Comparator (CC)* - This module allows users to automatically compare the different cloud providers based on the cost and configuration of the offered servers (which is stored in the provider catalog database), and the performance benchmarking results stored in the benchmark results database. *Report Generator* generates test reports in different formats including graphical, tabular and textual formats for consumption by both technical and non-technical users. *Visualizer* component allows users to visualize the test results and use different ranking and evaluation criteria to rank them.
- *Cloud Manager (CM)* - This module performs fundamental cloud resource management. *Instance Manager (IM)* procures appropriate instances on the different providers - both for the System Under Test (SUT) and the Test Agents (TA) based on the resource provisioning instructions from the BO. It is also responsible for the decommissioning of the instances at the end of each test. *Virtual Machine Image (VMI) Manager* is responsible for creating and maintaining virtual machine images on the different cloud providers. *Common Cloud Interface (CCI)* provides a common interface to different public cloud providers and enables the automated management of cloud instances including instantiation and termination.
- *Cloud Provider and Benchmark Catalogs* - Smart CloudBench maintains a catalog of supported IaaS providers and their offerings. It also maintains a catalog of supported benchmarks for the different types of representative applications.
- *Benchmark Results Database* - The results of the performance benchmarking are stored in the benchmark results database and can be used for analysing the evolution of cloud performance over time.

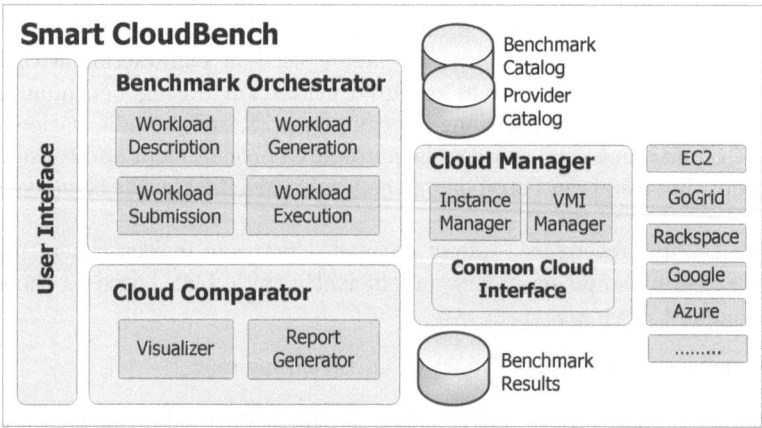

Fig. 1. Smart CloudBench architecture

– *User Interface (UI)* - The user interacts with Smart CloudBench through a browser-based UI (Fig. 1).

4   Using Smart CloudBench

In this section, we explain the steps involved in executing a typical benchmark using Smart CloudBench (see Fig. 2). We also include relevant screenshots to illustrate the usage scenarios (see Fig. 3).

– *Provider Selection* - In Step 1, the user selects the specific cloud providers and resource configurations to test. This selection is done based on user requirements, which could include resource configuration, cost, geographic location, supported operating systems etc.
– *Benchmark Selection* - In Step 2, the user selects the representative benchmark application/s from the list of available benchmarks that is to be used to evaluate the performance of the selected cloud server configurations.
– *Workload Specification* In Step 3, the user defines different scenarios to be tested against the selected benchmark. The request (comprising of the selected benchmark, test scenarios, and cloud servers to be tested) is submitted to the BO. The first and second steps can be used interchangeably.
– *Instance Procurement* - In Step 4, the BO receives the benchmarking request and directs the CM to procure the required cloud server instances from the

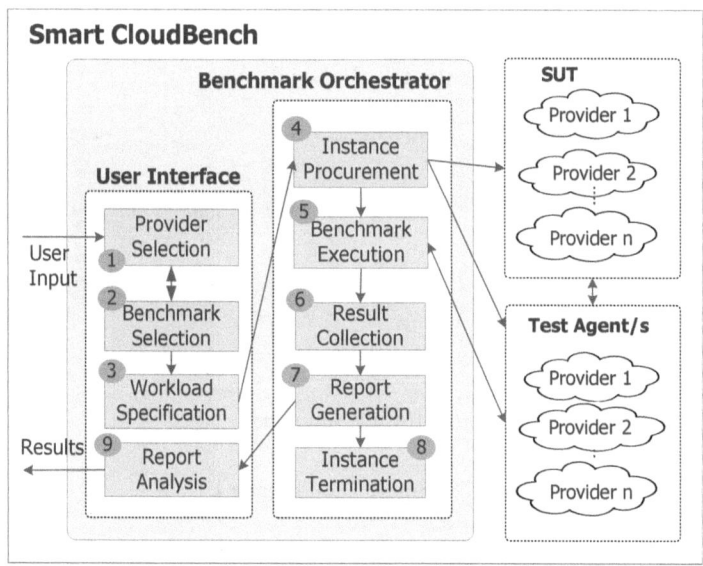

Fig. 2. Smart CloudBench workflow

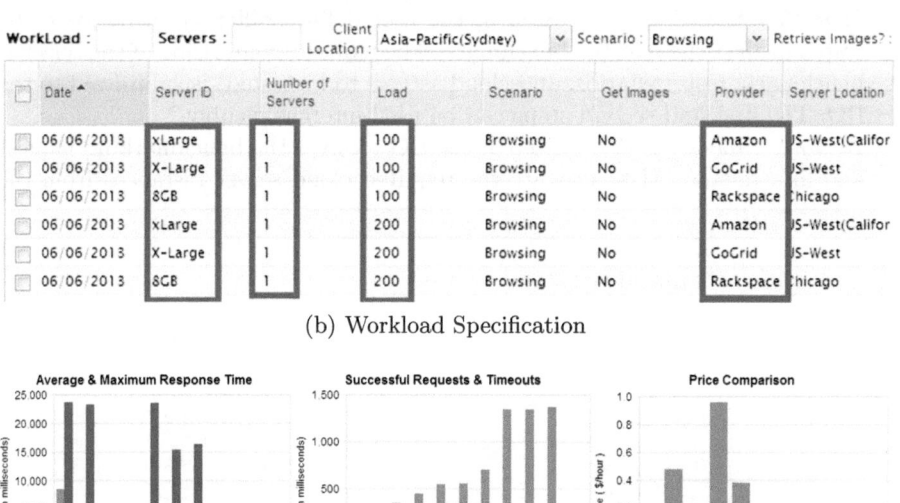

(a) Provider Catalog

(b) Workload Specification

(c) Result Summary

Fig. 3. Smart CloudBench UI

selected providers. Technically, the CM generates requests to the required
cloud provider's APIs in order to launch VMs with specific server configurations as specified in Step 1. Pre-built images containing the packaged applications are used to start up the SUT and the TA.

- *Benchmark Execution* - In Step 5, the BO executes the benchmark by issuing remote calls to the test agents running on the newly started cloud machines and waits for the benchmark results to be returned to it.
- *Result Collection* - On completion of the tests, the TAs return the benchmarking results to the BO in Step 6.
- *Report Generation and Visualisation* - In Step 7, the BO updates the Benchmark Results Database. The user can visualize the results either in tabular format or in graphical format. The reports combine the pricing and configuration information with the performance results. Users can use the test results for further analysis and decision-making.
- *Instance Decommissioning* - Once the tests have finished, the BO requests the CM to decommission the instances that were initally started up for the tests in Step 8.
- *Report Analysis* - In Step 9, the user can analyze the test results returned by Smart CloudBench.

5   Benchmarking Results

In this section, we describe the experimental environment we have used to demonstrate and validate the usefulness of Smart CloudBench. The representative benchmark application that we have used in our experiments is TPC-W [5], which simulates an on-line retail store. We have selected this particular application because it represents the most popular type of application running on the cloud and its behaviour is relatively simple and well understood. We first describe the experimental setup and the measured metrics followed by the results of the benchmarking tests performed on 3 different servers offered by a large IaaS provider in Australia.

5.1   TPC-W Benchmark

The TPC-W application models an online bookstore which is representative of a typical enterprise web application. It includes a web server to render the web pages, an application server to execute business logic, and a database to store application data. It is designed to test the complete application stack and does not make any assumptions about the technologies and software systems used in each layer. The benchmark consists of two parts. The first part is the TPC-W application which supports a mix of 14 different types of web interactions and three workload mixes, including searching for products, shopping for products and ordering products. The second part is the remote browser emulation (RBE) system which generates the workload to test the application. The RBE simulates the same HTTP network traffic as would be seen by a real customer using the browser. An open source implementation of TPC-W is available online.[3]

---

[3] Source code is available for both the TPC-W benchmark server implementation as well as the client implementation (TA) is available online at http://www.cs.virginia.edu/th8k/downloads/.

During each benchmarking cycle, the TPC-W client generates a random number of simultaneous requests to the server, depending on the specified number of emulated browsers. A single emulated browser can request only one web-page at a time. The client also simulates the waiting time between the browsing sessions of each emulated user. The server responds to the requests of the client by generating the corresponding web-pages. In case the request time exceeds 25 s, the request is dropped by timeout. The total number of requests that are made in a single benchmarking cycle varies depending on the response time. If the server cannot cope with the workload, the average response time and the number of timeouts will be high. In such case the number of generated requests will be lower, than when the server is capable of handling the generated workload and responds faster to the incoming requests.

5.2   Experimental Setup

We selected three large servers - 8GB, 16GB and 24GB servers (as shown in Table 1) to run the benchmark application on. The workload for each server was generated from separate test agents which operated on 24GB servers. Both the SUT and the TAs were located in Sydney. Workloads of 500 and 1000 concurrent clients were used to test the server performance over time. The benchmarking tests were run in parallel for 5 full days starting on Friday, 23/08/2013 at 6 pm and finishing on Wednesday, 28/08/2013 at 6 pm.

Table 1. Configurations of the instances used in the benchmarking experiments (prices correct on 23/08/2013)

Server	RAM (GB)	vCPU	Price (AUD/h)
S1	8	4	0.629
S2	16	8	1.246
S3	24	8	1.8

The benchmarking exercise was configured to run as follows. The duration of each benchmarking cycle was set at 5 min.; 2–2.5 min. for the benchmarking exercise and 2.5–3 min. pause before resuming the next round of testing. We paused at the end of each benchmarking cycle in order to minimise the impact of the congested server requests on the server performance in the next benchmarking cycle. As part of the benchmarking exercise, we collected the following metrics:

– Average Response Time (ART)
– Maximum Response Time (MRT)
– Total Number of Successful Interactions (SI)
– Total Number of Timeouts (T)

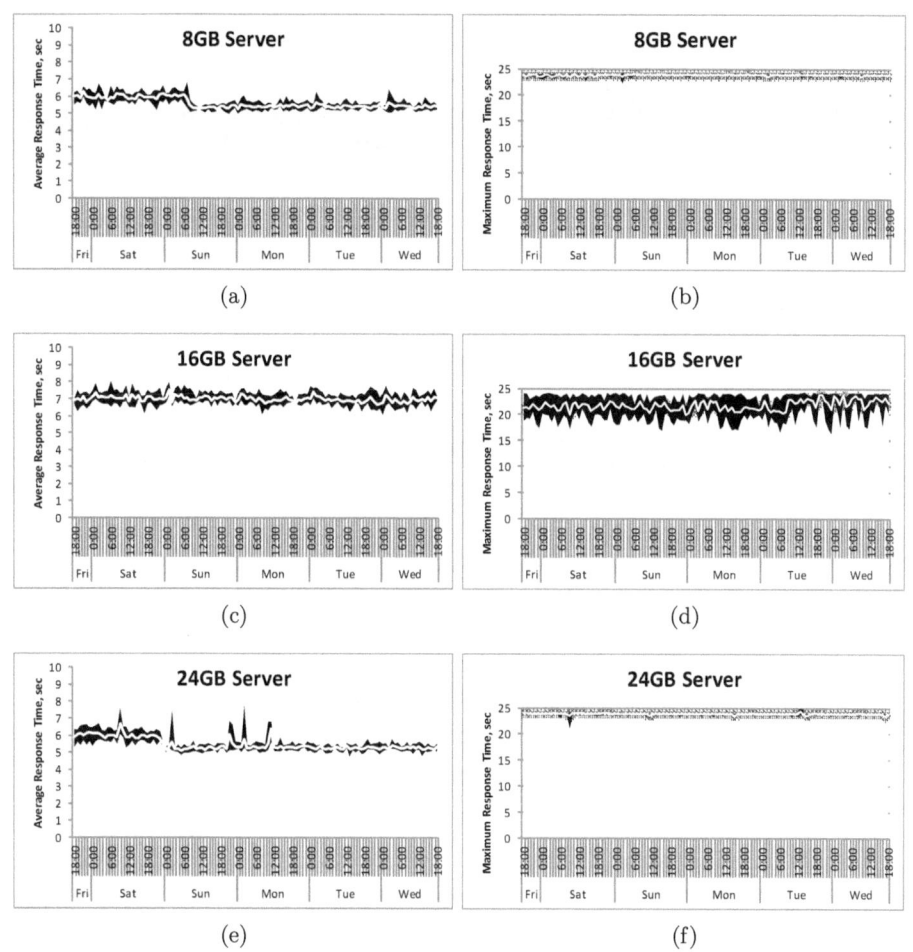

Fig. 4. Average and maximum response time (over time)

5.3   Discussion of Results

The results of the benchmarking exercise are presented in Figs. 4 and 5. The figures display the average response time, the maximum response time, the total number of successful interactions and the total timeouts, all measured over time. The black zones around the average figure (white line) represent the variance of performance in a particular hour. On analysing the benchmark results, we made the following observations.

- **Performance of 16GB server is significantly lower compared to that of 8GB and 24GB servers.** In Fig. 4 we can see that the ART of the 16GB server fluctuates consistently between 6 and 8 s. In contrast, 8GB and 24GB servers have a much better ART, which is on-average around 4 s until

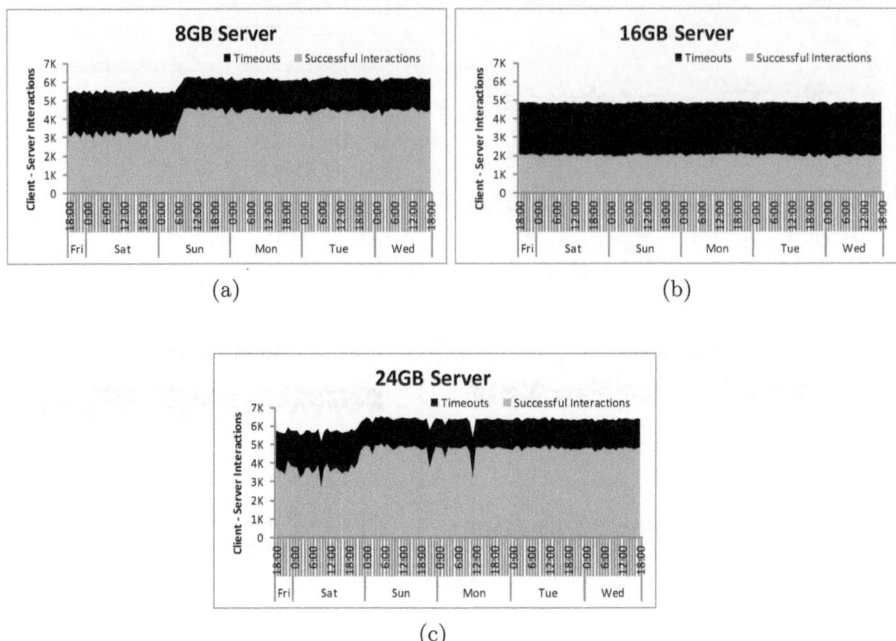

Fig. 5. Timeouts and successful interactions

Saturday midnight and then drops to around 2 s afterwards, showing improved performance. However, the 8 and 24GB servers do have several spikes, where the performance drops significantly, whereas the 16GB server shows more consistent performance. If we compare the price of the three servers, we can see that the 16GB server is nearly twice as costly as the 8GB server, and the 24GB server is nearly three times more expensive than the 8GB server. However, the performance of the 8GB server is better than that of the 16GB server and comparable with that of the 24GB server (for the workload of 500 and 1000 concurrent users). These results give a clear indication that making assumptions about the performance of cloud infrastructure based on the price and the specification is not a good decicion-making approach.

- **The server performance varies quite significantly over time.** We can observe that the performance of the 8 and 24GB servers improved significantly on Sunday; the ART dropped from 4 to 2 s and the total number of client-server interactions increased up to 1000 requests, while the number of requests timeouts dropped to insignificant value. A potential reason for such behaviour could be CPU bursting which is essentially the availability of additional CPU cycles due to less CPU contention.
- **When the workload increases the server performance becomes more predictive.** In the case of all three servers we can observe that when the workload increases, the deviation in server performance becomes smaller. Such

behaviour is most likely linked with the way the TPC-W client generates the requests to the server. As TPC-W simulates the real user behaviour, each emulated browser requests a web-page and waits for the server response before issuing another request to the server. Obviously, when the server is congested, it takes longer time to respond and fewer requests are generated in a single benchmarking cycle (about 150 s). As a consequence, it is possible that 500 and 1000 EBs can generate the same number of requests. We can see in the Fig. 5 that the 16GB server is overloaded and receives 2500 requests in total; however the 24GB server receives 5000 requests, which is twice more. Moreover, when the server is not capable to cope with the generated workload more requests are dropped by the timeout.

6   Related Work

There are a number of commercial and academic tools that provide support for cloud performance benchmarking. CloudHarmony[4] provides an extensive data-base of benchmark results for a fee across a number of public cloud providers using a wide range of benchmark applications. Cloud Spectator[5] is another provider which carries out periodic benchmarking and publishes the results in reports which can be purchased. ServerBear[6] measures CPU, IO, IOPS and network performance and provides customised reports against selected providers for a fee. Cedexis[7] offers tools for the real time monitoring of response times to over 100 cloud providers and Global Delivery Networks.

There are also several academic research projects in this area. CloudCmp [8] is a framework to compare cloud providers based on the performance of the various infrastructure components including computation, scaling, storage and network connectivity. CloudProphet [9] is a tool to predict the end-to-end response time of an on-premise web application when migrated to the cloud. CloudSuite [6] is a benchmark suite for emerging scale-out workloads. CloudRank-D [11] is a benchmark suite for benchmarking and ranking the performance of cloud computing systems hosting big data applications. SkyMark [7] is a tool that provides support for micro performance benchmarking in the context of multi-job workloads based on the MapReduce model. The Cloud Architecture Runtime Evaluation (CARE) framework [10] evaluates cloud platforms by using a number of pre-built, pre-configured and reconfigurable components for conducting performance evaluations across different target platforms.

There are three key features that differentiate Smart CloudBench from the other cloud performance benchmarking tools. The first feature is *real-time benchmarking* - users can conduct live, real-time benchmarking of selected cloud providers and servers (they can also make use of historical benchmark results). The second feature is the ability to *customize workloads*. Users are not restricted

---

[4] http://cloudharmony.com/benchmarks
[5] http://www.cloudspectator.com/
[6] http://serverbear.com/
[7] http://www.cedexis.com/products/radar.html

to pre-defined workloads but can instead specify workloads that are representative of their own in-house workloads making the benchmark results more meaningful and relevant. The third feature is the ability to do *performance baselining*. Users can baseline the performance of cloud servers against a wide range of workloads. This helps them select the cloud configuration and provider with the most appropriate specifications that best meet the user's requirements.

7   Conclusion

Prospective cloud consumers would like to obtain a quick assessment of the price, specification and performance of different IaaS providers before making any migration decisions. While the pricing and specification is public information, the performance of computing infrastructure is unknown. The use of different virtualization technologies by cloud providers impacts the performance of software systems running on top of the their infrastructure. The only way to get a measure of cloud infrastructure performance is by benchmarking software systems on it rather than relying on assumptions based on price and specification. In this paper, we have presented Smart CloudBench, which allows the automated execution of representative benchmarks on different IaaS clouds under representative load conditions to quickly estimate their performance levels. It helps decision-makers make informed decisions about migrating their in-house systems to the cloud by evaluating available options based on their price, specification and performance. Users of Smart CloudBench can design different types of experiments to test the performance of representative applications using load conditions that match the load levels of their own in-house applications. Smart CloudBench is particularly useful for organizations that do not possess the time, resources and in-house expertise to do a thorough evaluation of multiple cloud platforms. Tests conducted using it show that higher price does not necessarily translate to better or more consistent performance and highlight the need for tools such as Smart CloudBench to provide greater visibility into cloud infrastructure performance and to aid in the cloud migration decision-making process.

Acknowledgment. This work was partially funded by the Service Delivery and Aggregation Project within the Smart Services CRC.

References

1. Baruwal Chhetri, M., Vo, Q.B., Kowalczyk, R., Lan Do, C.: Cloud broker: helping you buy better. In: Bouguettaya, A., Hauswirth, M., Liu, L. (eds.) WISE 2011. LNCS, vol. 6997, pp. 341–342. Springer, Heidelberg (2011)
2. Baruwal Chhetri, M., Chichin, S., Vo, Q.B., Kowalczyk, R.: Smart CloudBench: automated performance benchmarking of the cloud. In: Proceedings of CLOUD 2013, 27 June–2 July 2013, California (2013)

3. Baruwal Chhetri, M., Vo, Q.B., Kowalczyk, R.: Policy-based automation of SLA establishment for cloud computing services. In: Proceedings of the 11th IEEE/ACM International Symposium on Cluster, Cloud and Grid Computing (CCGRID-12), Ottawa (Canada), 13–16 May 2012

4. Baruwal Chhetri, M., Vo, Q.B., Kowalczyk, R.: AutoSLAM - a policy-driven middleware for automated SLA establishment in SOA environments. In: Proceedings of the 9th International Conference on Service Computing (SCC 2012), Honolulu, Hawaii, USA, pp. 9–16. IEEE (2012)

5. Transaction Processing Performance Council. TPC Benchmark W (Web Commerce) Specification, version 2.0r. Technical Specification (2003). http://www.tpc.org/tpcw/spec/TPCWV2.pdf

6. Ferdman, M., et al.: Clearing the clouds: a study of emerging scale-out workloads on modern hardware. In: The 17th International Conference on Architectural Support for Programming Languages and Operating Systems (2012)

7. Iosup, A., Prodan, R., Epema, D.: IaaS cloud benchmarking: approaches, challenges, and experience. In: Proceedings of 5th Workshop on Many-Task Computing on Grids and Supercomputers (MTAGS) (2012)

8. Li, A., Yang, X., Kandula, S., Zhang, M.: CloudCmp: comparing public cloud providers. In: Proceedings of the 10th Annual Conference on Internet Measurement, November 2010

9. Li, A., Yang, X., Kandula, S., Yang, X., Zhang, M.: CloudProphet: towards application performance prediction in cloud. In: Proceedings of ACM SIGCOMM 2011, Toronto, pp 426–427 (2011)

10. Zhao, L., Liu, A., Keung, J.: Evaluating cloud platform architecture with the care framework. In: Proceedings of 17th APSEC, pp. 60–69 (2010)

11. Luo, C., et al.: CloudRank-D: benchmarking and ranking cloud computing systems for data processing applications. Front. Comput. Sci. **6**(4), 347–362 (2012)

A Six Cell Services Comparison Model
for Healthcare

Saradhi Motamarri[✉]

School of Information Systems, Technology and Management,
Australian School of Business, University of New South Wales,
Sydney, NSW, Australia
saradhi.motamarri@unsw.edu.au

Abstract. Healthcare services delivery is particularly complex. Understanding patients' perception and channeling those factors into services design and operation enhances sustainability. For its survival, a service must perform better than competition. Comparison with competition is a core element of House-of-Quality. There are isolated studies focused on single service systems, and very few studies on inter-system comparison. In the quest to identify the distinguishing factors of mHealth from other conventional services, the author realized the pressing need for a systematic model to relatively position comparison studies. Services comparison vis-à-vis competition is vital for services innovation. To fill this gap in literature, a *Six Cell Services Comparison Model* (SCSCM) is proposed and is applied to a few studies related to healthcare. The outcomes of services comparison, provides vital measures for improved and efficient design of services that meet and fulfill patients' needs, and hence contribute to quality healthcare.

Keywords: Healthcare · (SCSCM) · House of Quality (HoQ) · Services design · Mobile health (mHealth)

1 Introduction

In the quest to address healthcare challenges of the developing world [1, 2], the author has identified that there are three significant research opportunities for services science and in healthcare sector. These broad themes can be summarized as:

1. Services Life Cycle Model
2. Services Design; and
3. Services Comparison.

In manufacturing, finance and other services industries, continual innovation has brought newer forms of delivery giving rise to newer forms of services [3]. Competition in healthcare delivery has led to the evolution of services like: outpatient surgery centers, executive wellness programs, independent nursing group practices, hospitals, nursing homes, intermediate care facilities and home healthcare programs [4]. Mobile Health (mHealth) is one of the emerging alternatives to this range of healthcare services [1]. Motamarri [1] has analyzed mHealth with respect to conventional healthcare

J.G. Davis et al. (Eds.): ASSRI 2013, LNBIP 177, pp. 74–84, 2014.
DOI: 10.1007/978-3-319-07950-9_6, © Springer International Publishing Switzerland 2014

services, i.e., general practitioner (GP), public hospital (PH), and traditional medicine (TM). Motamarri et al. [2] provides a quantitative comparison of mHealth and conventional services from patients' perspective. The study extracted the distinguishing factors of mHealth with the aid of *multiple discriminant analysis* (MDA). In due course of these investigations, the author has identified the need for a model to relatively position comparison studies. Furthermore, the model must span the comprehensive spectrum of comparisons to comprehend extant literature and establish avenues for future research. If the model happens to be domain independent, then this as well can be applied to other domains, and becomes a valuable artifact for services science. This paper focuses on the development and brief application of such a model, termed as, a *Six Cell Services Comparison Model* (SCSCM).

2   Methods

A literature search has been made in various sources like PubMed, Google Scholar, and SciVerse databases for studies devoted to healthcare services design or comparison (*patient-service provider interaction*). A reconnaissance of the results has not pointed to any suitable artifacts relating to healthcare services design or comparison. The author has noted that the *Agency for Healthcare Research and Quality* (AHRQ) of the US Department of Health and Human Services has made significant contributions to improve quality, safety, efficiency and effectiveness of healthcare for the Americans. The AHRQ supports research that helps people make more informed decisions and improves the quality of healthcare services. The School of Design and Carnegie Mellon University has contributed towards design research pertaining to healthcare facilities to improve the patient flows and the patients' experience of healthcare environments [5].

Services design, provision and operation are essentially multi-disciplinary in nature [6]. Considering the complexity and inter-disciplinary nature of this endeavor, the research calls for the assimilation of knowledge from several disciplines. Following this multi-disciplinary search in terms of healthcare services in developing countries converging to healthcare services comparison, spanning the knowledge domains of ICT, Quality of Service, *IT Infrastructure Library* (ITIL) and *House of Quality* (HoQ) has provided interesting insights. As this is a significant opportunity that can benefit healthcare service providers as well as researchers, these insights will be reviewed towards developing a framework for services comparison.

The study of the extant literature revealed that three distinct streams play a pivotal role in addressing the significant shortcomings of the developing world, i.e. the provision of healthcare to the underserved and unserved segments across the globe [1]. The three aspects are: ICT/Mobile Communications, healthcare services quality in the developing world and services science. The finer elements of individual disciplinary streams are portrayed in Fig. 1. A detailed discussion of these elements is beyond the scope of this paper, and interested readers can refer to [1].

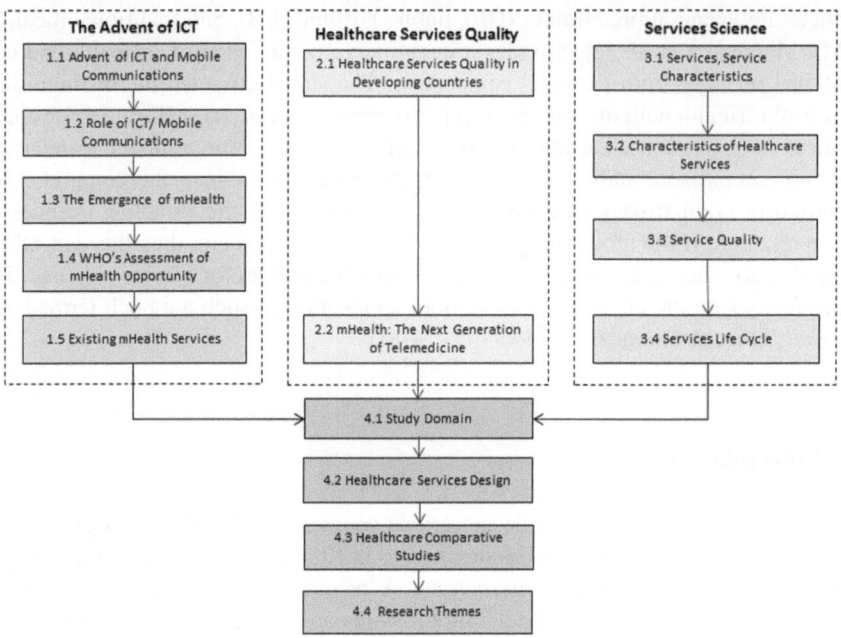

Fig. 1. Healthcare services comparison – a multi-disciplinary investigation, source: [1]

3 The Need for Healthcare Services Design Framework

Considering the broad agenda of better healthcare for all and the dire situation of healthcare status in developing countries [2, 7] there is a significant opportunity for the research community to direct attention toward services design and services operation. However, there is a paucity of studies on how to bring the patients' perspective to the service providers and guide them in devising healthcare services. Our multi-disciplinary search pointed us to *House of Quality* (HoQ) and *IT Infrastructure Library* (ITIL) as potential tools to this end. ITIL [8] provides a systematic framework to address the services operation phase. While ITIL focuses on the operational aspect of Services Management, HoQ essentially deals with the design of products and services.

Deming's famous PDCA Cycle is the underlying foundation for QFD and ITIL. HoQ is a basic design tool and part of the management approach *Quality Function Deployment* (QFD). Hauser and Clausing's [9] classic paper on HoQ, has brought its significance to the worldwide community. With its wide spread success in bringing together various functional divisions of manufacturing, HoQ has been applied in various forms and to various degrees of sophistication in manufacturing, engineering and subsequently in the design of services [10, 11]. HoQ inter-links customer requirements, their rankings, engineering characteristics, performance measures, competitive products/services and thereby elicits in a single diagram the areas of improvements required to win in the market.

The HoQ Matrix consists of eight rooms, each room exemplifying a stage of service design [10, 12]. HoQ not only helps in the design of products/services but also in drawing conclusions about their *competitive position in the market*. This comparative evaluation of the market helps in examining the strengths and weaknesses and thereby helps in product/services positioning. It also directs in devising an action plan to bridge any of the identified deficiencies [12]. In the event, a service provider ignores these competitive insights; Keaveney's model [13] suggests that the customers may switch providers thereby either leading to the eventual decline or disappearance of a product/service from the market. In either case, both HoQ and Keaveney's models emphasize the importance of comparative analysis of services. A good service design and consistent operation of the service are essential to raise the bar of user satisfaction [8].

Within the healthcare realm, scholars have investigated patient perceptions of service quality in general [14–20] and mHealth in particular [21]. While there has been research on the aspects of service quality of mHealth from patients' perspective [21–24], they have not addressed how mHealth is different from other healthcare services. These lessons provided motivation to search the literature for comparative analysis of healthcare services. In the extant literature there are very few studies devoted to the comparison of healthcare services. And there are hardly any studies devoted to a comparative analysis of mHealth with respect to other healthcare alternatives.

4   A Six Cell Services Comparison Model (SCSCM)

Services delivery is challenging. Services marketing and management pose special challenges because services deal with 'processes rather than things, with performances more than physical objects' [25]. Three management functions – marketing, operations and human resources – are intimately joined in what Lovelock has dubbed the '*service trinity*,' to create and deliver services. Healthcare services are even more complex due to the inherent nature of their dealing with people's health and survival. As noted before, service providers shall constantly need to understand their value proposition vis-à-vis competition. It is essential for both healthcare service providers as well as regulators to understand and measure the perceptions of the patients with respect to the services they receive in the market place. To fill this gap in the extant literature, the author proposes a *Six Cell Services Comparison Model* (SCSCM) as shown in Fig. 2.

In the broadest sense, patients' perceptions and comparison of competing services can be performed both at qualitative and quantitative levels. So the model considers this as vertical axis. On the other hand, the studies can be devoted into:

(i)   A sole service (GP, PH, TM or mHealth);
(ii)   A set of services within a system (intra-system i.e., hospital vs. hospital); or
(iii) Services across a broad spectrum of inter-systems (GP vs. mHealth).

So there is a possibility for three categories of comparison along the horizontal axis, namely: *single system*, *intra-system* and *inter-system*. Thus, the combination of

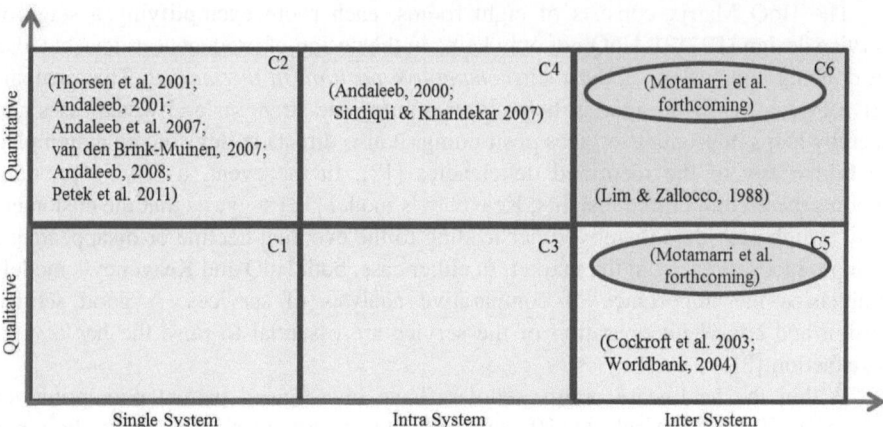

Fig. 2. Six cell services comparison model (SCSCM)

three categories along the horizontal and two divisions on the vertical axis, gives rise to six cells as shown in the Fig. 2. The cells are numbered from C1 to C6. The model also highlights the original investigation, i.e., *Quantitative Inter-System Comparison* (C6) that has led the author to the formulation of this model. In the extant literature, there are very few studies devoted to inter-system comparison (C5 and C6). Furthermore, researchers have considered many aspects of mHealth, but it is scarce to see a comparative study of mHealth vis-à-vis conventional services.

Historically, physicians are used to act as surrogate decision makers for the patient. However, with drastic changes in healthcare this model is replaced by a consumer centric model which recognizes the patient's increasing role in both influence and selection stages of the healthcare decision process [4, 26, 27]. The next sub-sections will look into a couple of studies devoted to general practice, hospitals and then move on to inter-system studies. Figure 2 also plots some of these studies on the SCSCM classification scale. These comparison studies facilitate in finding distinguishing characteristics of different services that separate them from each other.

4.1 Patients' Evaluation of General Practice

Ascertaining and promotion of quality in general practice (GP) and primary care is not only a necessity but also essential in retaining the service portfolio. The continual assessment helps to alter and tailor the services to suit to the consumers [18]. Similar motivations have driven Thorsen et al. [19] to study the purpose of GP consultation from the patients' perspective. Other researchers like van den Brink-Muinen et al. [28] have explored the basic question of whether doctors' talks with patients meet the patients' expectations. They observe that patients want an attentive, friendly, frank, and empathetic doctor who listens well of their bio-medical concerns and advises and tries to alleviate their issues. As these studies primarily devoted to a particular healthcare service, i.e. GP and they are quantitative in nature, these studies belong to Cell-2 of SCMCS.

Petek et al. [17] have performed a longitudinal survey (n = 7472) in which they have collected patients' evaluations of European General Practice. The respondents are chronic care illness patients. The research objective is to compare patients' evaluation of the current study of 2009 with a previous similar study done in 1998. They have used EUROPEP questionnaire consisting of 23-items. Petek et al. have not found any major changes between the 1998 and 2009 for all the countries combined. More than 80 % of the patients rated GPs most positively (4 or 5 on the Likert scale). However, they are not happy on the factors: waiting time (72.1 %), telephone accessibility (82.7 %), and dealing with emotional problems (83.2 %). Petek et al. found accessibility over phone to GP and waiting time are important determinants of the healthcare system satisfaction. Incidentally, mHealth can alleviate accessibility, availability and waiting time issues.

The other important conclusion which comes out of the Petek et al. study is that there is no good correlation between patients' assessments of the quality of care and the respective biomedical outcomes. Similar observations are also made by other researchers based on their patient satisfaction studies in relation to total hip arthroplasty [29]. Finally, Petek et al. conclude that service providers must aim for complete patient satisfaction; else there is a chance that patients change their physician. This conclusion affirms that of the Keaveney's model that the consumers may switch providers if a better service alternative is available.

4.2   Intra-System Comparisons

Andaleeb [30] has studied quality of services provided by public and private hospitals in Bangladesh. He notes that large segments of the population in developing countries are deprived of a fundamental right: access to basic health care. Quoting a World Bank 1987 study, he observes that the situation is acute in Bangladesh as only 30 % of the population has access to primary health care. Due to the Bangladesh government's regulatory reforms during 1982–1996, there was an increase of 346 private hospitals and 5,500 beds. Though there are signs of improvement in numbers in capacity, there is dearth of information with regard to quality of the services offered by hospitals. Public hospitals being subsidized by the government have marginal tendency to improve their services, while private hospitals which primarily run on patients' patronage are obligated to improve their services and be competitive among peers. As these quantitative studies focus on hospital systems, these studies are classified as Cell-4 of SCSCM.

To gauge patients' assessments of the hospital services they have received in the past, Andaleeb has used a modified framework to that of SERVQUAL of Parasuraman et al. [31]. Through qualitative interviews, Andaleeb established that a prominent cultural concept, *baksheesh* (facilitation payments) was prevalent in Bangladesh and needs to be included in the modified framework. He applied 2 group discriminant analysis (DA) to determine whether: service quality ratings (along with education and income) predicted choice of hospitals; and which factors accounted most for the differences in the scores; and how reliably the patients could be grouped into public or private hospital users.

The DA identified one significant discriminant function that produced a classification accuracy of 70.16 %. The accuracy is 25 % greater than that obtained by chance [32, 33] confirming a satisfactory predictive power of the model. Private hospitals were evaluated better on responsiveness, communication and discipline. The outcomes supported Andaleeb's premise that market incentives would explain differences in perceived quality of services provided by public and private hospitals. He observes that as the private hospitals' level of service has not measured up to the satisfaction of some of the affordable patients, they are switching to services in foreign countries thus costing the economy on the foreign exchange front. This implies that there is vast opportunity to improve healthcare services in Bangladesh. It can be noted that the emergence of mHealth service as a favorable alternative in Bangladesh [34] is not a major surprise due to the prevailing structural failure of the healthcare delivery in Bangladesh. This conclusion is well supported by a detailed study undertaken by the World Bank on the status of health services in developing countries [35].

Moving forward on the works of Andaleeb, Siddiqui and Khandaker [36] compared services of public and private hospitals of Bangladesh and then compared private hospitals with foreign counterparts from the perspective Bangladesh patients. They have quoted several prior studies that essentially concluded that public hospitals are used 30 % or lower due to the facts of unavailability of doctors and nurses, their attitudes and behavior, lack of drugs, waiting time, travel time etc. Their analysis showed that private hospitals were doing better in terms of availability of drugs, tangibility, perceived costs, empathy of nurses and responsiveness. It has also been derived that foreign hospitals are doing even better on these dimensions compared to private hospitals. Public hospitals also fared lower in the aspects of tangibility compounded by the factors of cleanliness, water supply, and availability of equipment. The cost has been treated as the patients' perception of costs that includes consultation, diagnostics, accommodation etc. Based on their analysis they concluded that the overall quality of service was better in foreign hospitals than the private hospitals in Bangladesh in all the factors, including 'perceived cost' factor.

4.3   Inter-System Comparisons

Lim and Zallocco [4] for the first time studied inter-system competition by analyzing the consumer attitudes toward divergent healthcare systems, namely: hospitals, home healthcare, nursing homes, and outpatient clinics. Their research objectives are:

- to determine consumer attitudes toward the four healthcare delivery systems;
- to determine how consumers' perceptions of these systems vary on specific attributes; and
- to identify dimensions that most clearly discriminate the four systems.

Lim and Zallocco conducted a survey in which respondents were questioned about their attitudes toward four healthcare delivery systems along 10 attributes: quality of medical care, safety, speed of recovery, quality of medical personnel, risk of complications, cleanliness, convenience, comfort, privacy provided, and cost. As this quantitative study focuses on different healthcare services, it belongs to Cell-6 of the SCSCM model.

Overall mean scores put hospitals as more safe, clean and of better quality. However, hospitals are perceived as more expensive. Nursing homes have the most negative image with respondents. In terms of lowest cost, outpatient clinics are rated more positively. On the dimensions of convenience, comfort, privacy and likelihood of speedy recovery, home health care is most positively rated. They performed MDA to classify the services. Lim and Zallocco found that the three dimensions: personalized care, quality of medical care and value distinguish the four healthcare services. MDA provided insights on which dimensions a particular service was positively viewed thereby providing useful inputs for service providers, healthcare researchers and policy makers. For example, home healthcare service providers can highlight their strengths as perceived by consumers in comfort, privacy, medical quality and likelihood of speedy recovery as differentiating factors to offer better services.

Motamarri et al. [2] have analyzed the distinguishing factors of mHealth in developing countries vis-à-vis three other conventional services: GPs, public hospitals and traditional medicine. To begin they have analyzed these services on a qualitative scale, conforming to Cell-5 of SCSCM. They conducted a quantitative survey and gathered patients' perceptions about mHealth and conventional services, conforming to Cell-6. They applied MDA to classify these services. Their analysis provided interesting comparative advantages of mHealth along three distinct attribute directions, namely, *ubiquity, information-quality and value.* The three attribute bundles extracted by MDA consisted of 11 sub-elements. This investigation not only filled a substantial gap in the literature on inter-system comparative studies, but also demonstrated for the first time, how mHealth is perceived significantly better than other alternatives in a developing country, i.e., Bangladesh.

5 Discussion

The review of healthcare services in developing countries, mHealth and HoQ has brought to fore the importance of services comparison and design. It is possible to draw a comparative analysis of existing healthcare services from both qualitative and quantitative perspectives. As the patients are the ultimate consumers of these services, it is essential to understand how patients perceive different healthcare services. Such research endeavors can answer from the patients' perspective:

1. Are different healthcare services distinguishable from each other?
2. Is mHealth (or for any service) distinct from other existing services? and
3. If so, what factors contribute to the service differentiation?

The answers to these questions are crucial for services design. Furthermore, it is also essential to understand the scope of this comparison and how it fits into the overall comparison spectrum. To this end the proposed SCSCM is a significant contribution not only to healthcare services but also to services in general.

5.1 Limitations/Future Research

This study has some limitations. There are opportunities to perform a comprehensive review of the literature to identify qualitative and quantitative studies pertaining to Cells-1, 2, 3 & 5. However, the main thrust has been Cell-6, i.e. quantitative studies devoted to inter-system comparison. Future research can be directed to consider this broad and impactful opportunity.

5.2 Conclusions/Research Contribution

The discussion emphasized the need for a robust healthcare services design framework. One of the key aspects of HoQ services design is *evaluation of competing services*. There is a vast research opportunity for comparative assessment of healthcare services. With this motivation the current investigation proposed a *Six Cell Services Comparison Model* (SCSCM). The application of SCSCM is briefly discussed for the set of studies, identified in a multi-disciplinary search (Fig. 1). Though the application of the proposed model focused on healthcare services, the model itself does not make any domain specific assumptions. Thus, the SCSCM model is generic and is of significant value for other service domains as well. The author thus hopes that the model generates interest and motivation and which in turn, shall pave way for better services.

References

1. Motamarri, S.: Distinguishing mHealth from other health care alternatives in developing countries: a study on service characteristics. Dissertation, School of Information Systems, Technology and Management, The University of New South Wales, Sydney, Australia, pp. 1–191 (2013)
2. Motamarri, S., Akter, S., Ray, P., Tseng, C.-L.: Distinguishing 'mHealth' from other healthcare services in a developing country: a study from the service quality perspective. Commun. Assoc. Inf. Syst. **34**, Article 34, 669–692 (2014)
3. Hwang, J., Christensen, C.M.: Disruptive innovation in health care delivery: a framework for business-model innovation. Health Aff. **27**(5), 1329–1335 (2008)
4. Lim, J.S., Zallocco, R.: Determinant attributes in formulation of attitudes toward four health care systems. J. Health Care Mark. **8**(2), 25–30 (1988)
5. Evenson, S.: Design thinking for innovative healthcare service. In: AHRQ Annual Conference, 08 Sept 2008 (2008)
6. Ghose, A.: Services research in Australia: a roadmap. In: Australian Symposium on Services Research and Innovation, Sydney (2012)
7. Economist: Squeezing out the doctor. In: The Economsit 2012, The Economist Newspaper Limited, London (2012)
8. OGC, ITIL, Version 3, Office of Government Commerce, The Stationery Office, London (2007)
9. Hauser, J.R., Clausing, D.: The house of quality. Harvard Bus. Rev. **66**(3), 63–73 (1988)
10. Ray, P.K.: Integrated Management from E-Business Perspective: Concepts, Architectures and Methodologies. Kluwer, New York (2003)

11. Ramaswamy, R.: Design and Management of Service Processes: Keeping Customers for Life. Addison-Wesley, Reading (1996)
12. Dieter, G., Schmidt, L.: Engineering Design, 4th edn. McGraw-Hill, New York (2008)
13. Keaveney, S.M.: Customer switching behavior in service industries: an exploratory study. J. Mark. 59(2), 71–82 (1995)
14. Heje, H.N., Olesen, F.: Patients' evaluations as quality measurements in general practice. Ugeskr. Laeger 164(46), 5386–5389 (2002)
15. Andaleeb, S.S.: Service quality perceptions and patient satisfaction: a study of hospitals in a developing country. Soc. Sci. Med. 52(9), 1359–1370 (2001)
16. Andaleeb, S.S., Siddiqui, N., Khandakar, S.: Patient satisfaction with health services in Bangladesh. Health Policy Plann. 22(4), 263–273 (2007)
17. Petek, D., et al.: Patients' evaluations of European general practice—revisited after 11 years. Int. J. Qual. Health Care 23(6), 621–628 (2011)
18. Ramsay, J., et al.: The General Practice Assessment Survey (GPAS): tests of data quality and measurement properties. Fam. Pract. 17(5), 372–379 (2000)
19. Thorsen, H., et al.: The purpose of the general practice consultation from the patient's perspective—theoretical aspects. Fam. Pract. 18(6), 638–643 (2001)
20. Ware, J.E.J., et al.: Consumer perceptions of health care services: implications for academic medicine. Acad. Med. 50(9), 839–848 (1975)
21. Akter, S., D'Ambra, J., Ray, P.: User perceived service quality of m-Health services in developing countries. In: 18th European Conference on Information Systems (2010)
22. Akter, S. Ray, P.: mHealth - An Ultimate Platform to Serve the Unserved. IMIA Yearbook of Medical Informatics, pp. 94–100. Schattauer, Germany (2010)
23. Akter, S., D'Ambra, J., Ray, P.: Service quality of mHealth platforms: development and validation of a hierarchical model using PLS. Electron. Markets 20(3), 209–227 (2010)
24. Akter, S., D'Ambra, J., Ray, P.: Trustworthiness in mHealth information services: an assessment of a hierarchical model with mediating and moderating effects using partial least squares (PLS). J. Am. Soc. Inform. Sci. Technol. 62(1), 100–116 (2011)
25. Lovelock, C., Wirtz, J.: Services Marketing: People, Technology, Strategy, 7th edn. Prentice Hall, Boston (2010)
26. Berkowitz, E.N., Hillestad, S.G.: Evolution of tripartite model of hospital selection. In: Procdings from Advances in Health Care Research, Association for Consumer Research (1982)
27. Wright, N.D., Parsons, R.J.: Consumers' selection of hospital maternity care. In: Proceedings from Advances in Health Care Research, Association for Consumer Research, Snowbird, UT (1982)
28. van den Brink-Muinen, A., et al.: Do our talks with patients meet their expectations? J. Fam. Pract. 56(7), 559 (2007)
29. Haverkamp, D., et al.: The validity of patient satisfaction as single question in outcome measurement of total hip arthroplasty. J. Long Term Eff. Med. Implants 18(2), 145–150 (2008)
30. Andaleeb, S.S.: Public and private hospitals in Bangladesh: service quality and predictors of hospital choice. Health Policy Plann. 15(1), 95–102 (2000)
31. Parasuraman, A., Zeithaml, V.A., Berry, L.L.: SERVQUAL: a multiple-item scale for measuring consumer perceptions. J. Retail. 64(1), 12–40 (1988)
32. Malhotra, N.: Marketing Research: An Applied Orientation, 4th edn. Pearson Education, Upper Saddle River (2004)
33. Hair, J.F.J., et al.: Multivariate Data Analysis: A Global Perspective, 7th edn. Pearson Prentice Hall, Upper Saddle River (2010)

34. Ivatury, G., Moore, J., Bloch, A.: A doctor in your pocket: health hotlines in developing countries. Innovations Technol. Gov. Globalization **4**(1), 119–153 (2009)
35. World Bank: World Development Report: Making Services Work for Poor People. World Bank, New York (2004)
36. Siddiqui, N., Khandaker, S.A.: Comparison of services of public, private and foreign hospitals from the perspective of Bangladeshi patients. J. Health Popul. Nutr. **25**(2), 221–230 (2007)

Decisions, Models and Opportunities in Cloud Computing Economics: A Review of Research on Pricing and Markets

Sowmya Karunakaran$^{(\boxtimes)}$, Venkataraghavan Krishnaswamy,
and R.P. Sundarraj

Department of Management Studies, IIT Madras, Chennai 600033, India
sowmya.karu@gmail.com, raghavan1980@yahoo.co.in, rpsundarraj@iitm.ac.in
http://www.doms.iitm.ac.in

Abstract. Cloud computing has emerged as a key information technology and systems model over the last few years. Major organizations have developed and delivered cloud computing solutions and continue to do so. Consequently, a number of strides were made in the advancement of technology leading to a growth in the adoption of cloud computing. The growing recognition of cloud computing services necessitates a focus on the business aspects of cloud. However, we feel that research in this area is scant. To this effect, we performed a systematic review of cloud computing literature and reviewed 2891 abstracts and 157 articles published until the year 2012. Based on the findings of the review, we establish a framework for organising the extant research on cloud business aspects. Using the framework, we find cloud economics to be the most widely researched business aspect. In this paper, we provide a detailed review of the application of decision models in the context of cloud economics, with a specific focus on pricing and markets. The proposed framework and review results serve as a reference to IS researchers and practitioners to understand decision situations, models and opportunities.

Keywords: Cloud computing · Utility computing · Decision models · Pricing · Markets · Review

1 Introduction

In the last few decades, technical research in IS contributed a number of parallel and distributed architecture based solutions [1]. Solutions like virtualisation and web-technologies coupled with continuing growth in hardware speed, decreasing costs of processing and storage and a dramatic increase in the number of computational devices has led to commoditization of computing resources popularly known as cloud computing. Cloud computing offers infrastructure, platform and software as a service (IaaS, PaaS and SaaS), and is envisioned to be the 5th utility [3]. With this movement to commoditization and forecasts of a market of

J.G. Davis et al. (Eds.): ASSRI 2013, LNBIP 177, pp. 85–99, 2014.
DOI: 10.1007/978-3-319-07950-9_7, © Springer International Publishing Switzerland 2014

size 241 billion USD [4] , ideas stemming from fields such as economics, management, and decision theory have become relevant to the new domain of computing. Research themes under economics include aspects such as pricing, markets, consumer behaviour, agent technology and so on. Studies on these aspects in particular have emerged and begun to mature. In terms of review studies, there are several works that provide review of themes pertaining to cloud. While most review works deal with taxonomy [5–10], few deal with detailed review of a specific focus area such as pricing [11] and adoption [12]. Further, most of extant research on cloud computing focuses on technology aspects and it is vital to look at economic aspects to bring in a holistic perspective to cloud computing discussions [13].

In our paper, we address these notions and specifically look into providing (1) a general classification framework for research pertaining to business features of cloud computing. (2) a detailed review of research on two streams under cloud economics namely, pricing and markets. The process of identifying the most widely researched business theme involved a systematic review of research on various business facets of cloud computing and classifying the identified research works. A review of business facets of cloud could typically benefit managers in an organizational setting and researchers in the IS space. In the course of decision making, organizations need to consider parameters relevant to the decision and use appropriate models and techniques to support their decision making. Researchers need to understand gaps, identify opportunities and address them suitably. Hence we organize our review discussion into three parts: decisions, models and research opportunities.

The organization of rest of this paper is as follows: In Sect. 2, we discuss previous literature reviews in cloud computing. In Sect. 3, we discuss the review methodology adopted in this study. In Sect. 4, we propose a classification framework and discuss in detail, two of the top researched areas under cloud economics, namely pricing and markets. In Sect. 5, we provide the implications and in Sect. 6, discuss the summary and limitations. Conclusions are presented in the last section.

2   Background

In this section, we provide a brief account of previous review studies in cloud computing and establish the motivation and the scope of our review. The following summary lists the various review studies pertaining to business and/or service aspects of cloud. Studies on technological aspects such as distributed computing frameworks and architectures, resource allocation technologies and autonomic management are beyond the scope of this paper.

2.1   Summary of Review Studies in Cloud

Literature review on business features of cloud computing are limited. Literature surveys have focused on (a) taxonomy of cloud services such as Infrastructure as a Service (IaaS), Platform-as-a-Service (PaaS) and Software-as-a-Service (SaaS)

[5, 9, 10], (b) classification based on technology, business, and applications [14], (c) classification based on service models and deployment modes namely public, private or hybrid [6], (d) classification based on license type, intended user group, security measures, standardization efforts and openness of cloud [11] and (e) state-of-the-art in cloud computing such as software frameworks, cloud architecture and security [15].

While, the aforementioned studies dealt with a broad morphology of cloud, few studies were specific to certain themes. Reference [11] dealt with a review of pricing models but the emphasis was on deriving a comparison across cloud and grid systems rather than the research review of cloud pricing literature. In [12], the authors provide a comparison of various cloud offerings and focus on building a decision framework but do not provide a comprehensive review of research pertinent to decision frameworks for the cloud. In [10], the authors provide a review and reference guide to Infrastructure as a Service type of cloud offering, but the focus is only on implications for e-Governance. Marston et al, provided a research agenda for business aspects of cloud [13].

An evaluation of review works on cloud indicates that (a) they lacked a systematic review approach and (b) they did not deal with decision situations/ models. A review of decisions and models is critical for the following reasons: (1) It acts as a basis for researchers to learn the state-of-the art, current challenges, enhance current models and propose solutions (2) It acts as a guide for practitioners to seek and apply such models. The extant literature is scant on review of decisions and models for organizational implications of cloud computing, particularly in densely researched areas such as cloud economics. This emphasizes the need for a systematic literature review.

2.2 Scope of Our Paper

We try to seek answers for two specific questions in our review. First, we try to understand the depth of research in terms of decision situations and models encompassing various business aspects of cloud computing. Second, we provide a discussion on top two widely researched areas focusing on decisions, models and opportunities for further research.

3 Methodology and Review Statistics

We looked at review studies from cloud computing and other domains to decide our review methodology. Our review methodology is adapted from systematic procedures followed in literature and includes planning and execution stages [2, 10, 16]. Following Kitchenham and other review studies, research objectives were framed as part of the planning stage. The research objectives are to identify (1) The business situations where decision models are applied and (2) Models and techniques used in modelling the decisions. As part of the execution stage, primary studies for the review were collected through a four step process. In the first step, 4207 articles were collected using a set of twenty one keywords and nine bibliographic databases (refer Table 1). All papers published until the year

Table 1. Keywords and databases

Keywords	Adoption, Allocation, Auction, Behaviour, Broker, Contract, Culture, Decision, Economics, Game, Market, Negotiation, Optimization, Partnership, Policy, Pricing, Regulation, Sourcing, Scheduling, SLA, Strategy
Databases	ACM, AIS, EBSCO, Emerald, Engineering Village IEEE, Scopus, Proquest

2012 were part of the screening process. The keywords were derived through a brainstorming session among the authors and was intended to capture various business dimensions of cloud computing. In the next step 1161 duplicates, 133 non-peer reviewed 22 non-cloud computing papers were eliminated, reducing the count to 2891 articles. The third and fourth steps were designed to ensure that selected articles meet the inclusion criteria. In accordance with the research objective, the inclusion criterion is defined as the application of a decision model towards the achievement of a business objective. The decision model could vary from a simple check-list to a complex mathematical model. Few trial reviews of abstracts ensured that the authors were on a common understanding. Subsequent to the review trials, in the third step, the authors divided the resultant 2891 papers among themselves and reviewed the abstracts to ensure that the paper met the inclusion criteria. As an outcome, 2317 papers were eliminated. In the fourth and final step, a joint review was performed to strengthen the selection process, reducing the count further down to 235 articles. However, 78 of these articles were inaccessible for complete download, limiting the full review to 157 papers. Figure 1 gives a snapshot of the review methodology and step-wise statistics.

The final set of 157 papers included 43 papers from 28 journals and 114 papers from 91 conferences as of December 2012. Figures 2 and 3 gives the top five journals and top five conferences based on the number of articles chosen from those journals and conferences. The disciplines that have contributed to decision models include techniques and models from economics, finance, operations, decision science and statistics. As part of our review, we have classified the decision models found in the 157 articles into 23 categories. The 23 categories were arrived by adapting categories from Marstonś framework [13] and through an analysis of keywords from the short-listed 157 articles.The subsequent section describes the proposed classification framework.

4   Classification Framework

We developed the Classification framework by adapting the framework proposed by Marston et al. [13]. In [13], the authors had divided IS research agenda in cloud computing into five broad areas: (1) Cloud Computing economics,

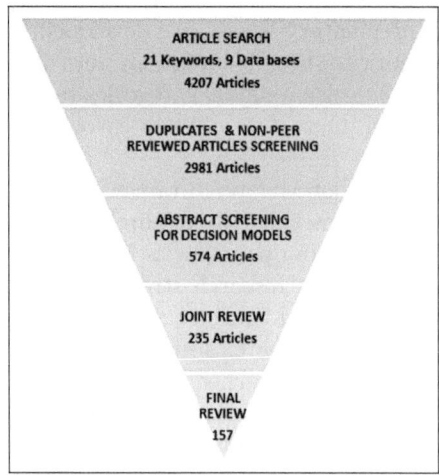

Fig. 1. Review methodology

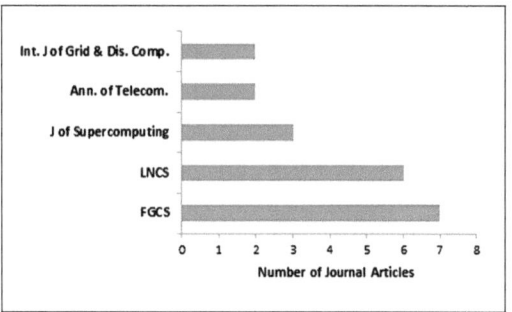

Fig. 2. Top 5 journals

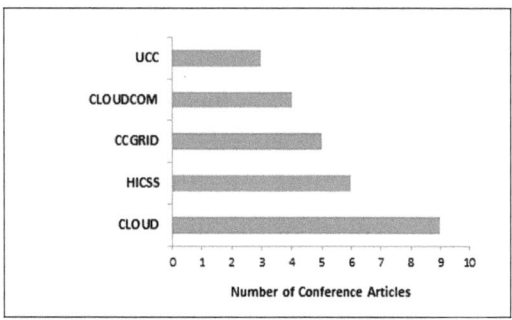

Fig. 3. Top 5 conferences

(2) Strategy research, (3) IS Policy research (4) Technology adoption and implementation research (5) Regulatory Issues. We developed this categorization further by adding sub categories. The sub-categories were essential to add a layer or resolution and map the 23 decision model categories to the five broad categories identified by Marston et al. Out of the 23 sub-categories, 12 were new and 11 were retained from Marstonś framework.

Table 2 gives an overview of Marstonś framework and sub-categories corresponding to 23 research streams. The 157 research articles were classified under 23 categories. The numbers within parenthesis in Table 2 denote the number of research papers classified in each research stream. A research paper may span across several research streams and hence could be categorised in more than one category. However, in such cases the closest classification was adopted. As the numbers indicate, Cloud economics turned out to be the widely researched area, while Pricing, Adoption, Sourcing, Market and Resource Allocation turned out to be the widely five researched streams at the sub category level. Our review will focus on the category *cloud economics* with emphasis on two of the widely research streams namely *pricing* and *markets*. Our review attempts to list (a) decision variables identified by various authors (b) summarize key works (c) research questions from the articles (d) research questions proposed by us and (e) popular techniques and models used.

4.1   Pricing

Pricing models help service providers to realise the value for services offered by them. Pricing includes setting the right tariffs and charging schemes. Review of research in pricing reveals four broad sub-themes: pricing schemes, user welfare, pricing elements and collaborative pricing. Table 3 summarizes key works in the area of pricing.

4.1.1   Decisions

Pricing Schemes: Researchers have widely studied pricing schemes such as pay-as-you-go and dynamic pricing. In [30], the authors discuss a dynamic pricing scheme suitable for allocating resources on federated clouds. In [18,19,26,35], the authors analysed dynamic pricing schemes through simulation based on real-time spot price data from a trace of Amazon EC2 spot market. In [31], the authors study the integration of currently deployed pricing schemes of real-world providers in the design of open markets. In [17], the authors propose that an optimally adjusted dynamic pricing model will outperform any pricing model with static prices. Certain studies have explored resource allocation mechanisms based on pricing. A new type of resource pricing and allocation policy proposes that users can predict resource price as well as satisfy budget and deadline constraints [34]. Bidding schemes and server allocation policies designed to optimize the average revenue earned by the SaaS provider per time unit were proposed [29]. An algorithm that takes cues from dynamic pricing and schedules the jobs/tasks in ways that the energy usage is low was developed [27]. In [33], the authors

Table 2. Classification framework

Marston's classification Broad areas	Added by authors Sub categories
Cloud economics (67)	**Pricing (32)**
	Markets (17)
	Sustainability (3)
	Agent technology (3)
	Brokering (4)
	Consumer behaviour(8)
Strategy issues in cloud (21)	Culture (1)
	Partnership (4)
	Fairness (4)
	Trust (9)
	Consumer preference (1)
	Consumer satisfaction (2)
IS Policy issues (48)	Interoperability (4)
	Sourcing (17)
	IT auditing (1)
	Security and privacy (8)
	Risk (10)
	SLA (4)
	Contract (4)
Technology adoption and implementation (41)	Cloud adoption (24)
	QoS (4)
	Resource allocation (13)
Regulatory (3)	Regulatory (3)

The numbers in brackets indicate the number of papers in that category

model bidding strategies for cloud resources in a dynamic pricing environment as a Prisoner Dilemma Game. [32] shows a method for pricing, developed using financial option theory where the cloud resources are treated as underlying assets to capture the realistic value of the cloud compute commodities.

User Welfare: Few authors have considered user welfare while designing or comparing pricing models. In [20], the authors propose a method to achieve social welfare in a cloud-computing environment through flat rate pricing using a congestion control approach. Another author has adopted the concept of pricing fairness from microeconomics and quantitatively analysed the impact of interference on pricing fairness [25].

Pricing Elements: Several authors have explored the elements to consider while deciding on pricing. The key elements for pricing included, hardware, maintenance, power, cooling, staff and amortization [36]. Additionally in [37], the authors have considered distribution of users, request bundle size and deadline constraints. A price update iterative algorithm, which analyses the historical utilization ratio of the resource and computes the price iteratively was developed [38]. In [21], the authors present a demand-based pricing model for maximizing revenue of data center providers that serve clients who aim to maximize their utilities using a game formulation.

Collaborative Pricing: Researchers have also started looking at collaborative pricing schemes to suit business models where the infrastructure resources are from multiple providers. For example, each user can bid a single price value for different composite/collaborative services provided by cloud providers and similarly the collaborating providers can set a common price for the collaborative services [23]. Another approach uses genetic algorithm for pricing in cloud markets, in which a naive pricing function evolves to a pricing function that offers suitable prices in function of the system status [28].

4.1.2   Models

A review of cloud pricing literature indicates the widespread use of game theoretic and simulation based models. Game theory was used to model demand based pricing as a Stackelberg game [21,22], bidding in online cloud markets as a Prisoner's Dilemma game [33], pricing in cloud banks and under constraints as a dynamic game [24,34] and achieving strategy proof resource pricing using mechanism design [30]. Simulation models were primarily used to model fluctuations in dynamic prices [17,19] and to test/compare performance parameters [20,37]. Few authors have employed techniques like Genetic Algorithm for addressing problems such as partner selection and price negotiation [23,28].

4.1.3   Research Gaps

From Literature: [34] enquired if the mechanisms for predicting price could be generalised and opined that the delay problems associated with price predictions cannot be addressed completely. In the case of dynamic pricing schemes, [30] questions if there is a trade-off between economics and efficiency? Can the bid price be optimized based on heuristics and learning algorithms [17]? On the other hand, there is a call for research on impact of user's bid price on dynamic pricing [26]. Though few works considered cost of energy as an important element of pricing, the cases where energy price changes hourly needs to be handled [27].

Proposed by Authors: Most works reviewed in this paper, have an implicit assumption that users are rational. However, cloud users could indeed have biases and consideration of these biases could be crucial while building pricing models. In addition, researchers need to consider improvements to pricing schemes, for example, inclusion of charge-back models to protect the consumer. Few researchers have introduced and discussed pricing models like the cloud bank model but researchers need to understand the disadvantages of these models and address them.

4.2   Markets

Cloud markets provide an electronic medium for trading resources [3]. They improve efficiencies and bring geographically distributed service providers and

Table 3. Pricing studies, themes and models

Author	Decision theme				Decision technique or model
	Pricing schemes	User welfare and fairness	Price elements	Collaborative pricing	
Anandasivam and Premm [17]	x				Simulation
Andrzejak et al. [18]	x				
Ben-Yehuda et al. [19]	x	x			Simulation
Li [20]	x	x	x		Simulation
Daoud et al. [21]	x		x		Game theory
Hadji et al. [22]	x	x			Game theory
Hassan et al. [23]				x	Genetic algorithm
Li and Li [24]			x	x	Game theory
Ibrahim et al. al. [25]		x			Machine learning
Javadi et al. [26]	x				Statistical model
Li and Lo [27]	x		x		Simulation
Macias and Guitart [28]				x	Genetic algorithm
Mazzucco and Dumas [29]	x				Heuristics
Mihailescu and Teo [30]	x	x			Game theory
Roovers et al. [31]	x				
Sharma et al. [32]	x				Financial options
Sowmya and Sundarraj [33]	x	x			Game theory
Teng and Magoules [34]	x	x			Game theory
Wee [35]	x				Regression
Woitaszek and Tufo [36]			x		
Zaman and Grosu [37]			x		Simulation

consumers onto a single platform. Cloud markets help avoid vendor lock-in, empower small vendors, aid infrastructure and platform and application innovation [39,40]. Review of research in cloud markets revealed the following decision themes: collaboration, welfare, strategy and design (See Table 4). The decision theme *collaboration* focuses on how services providers partner each other in offering cloud services. While collaboration is from the perspective of the service provider, decisions involving *welfare* concern all stakeholders, namely the buyer, the seller or an intermediary. The theme *strategy* discusses the mechanisms at the disposal of the service providers operating in the market. The theme *design* focuses on the requirements of a cloud market from an economic as well as a technological perspective, which essentially provides the framework to operate.

Table 4. Market studies, themes and models

Author	Decision theme				Decision technique or model
	Welfare	Strategy	Collaboration	Design	
Hassan et al. [23]			x		Optimization
Henzinger, T.A et al. [45]	x				Simulation
Breskovic et al. [44]	x				Machine learning
Garg et al. [46]	x			x	Simulation
Goiri et al. [41]			x	x	Simulation
You et al. [47]		x			Genetic algorithm
Chen and Yeh [43]	x				Optimization
Macias and Guitart [48]		x			Simulation
Fujiwara et al. [42]	x				Optimization
Breskovic et al. [49]				x	Simulation
Niyato et al. [50]		x			Game theory

4.2.1 Decisions

Collaboration: In [23], the authors propose a combinatorial auction based collective bidding mechanism where vendors can collaborate with each other to meet user requirements while reducing conflicts, costs and negotiation time. In [41], the authors describe the profits of a cloud service provider under outsourcing and in-sourcing conditions in a federated cloud environment.

Welfare: Decisions in welfare maximization, deal with solutions that benefit a seller as well as a buyer. In [42], a double-sided combinatorial auction with an objective of maximizing welfare in forward and spot cloud markets was formulated and solved as mixed integer program. In [43], the authors design a k-pricing based market mechanism to distribute the welfare between buyer and seller. In [44], the authors recommend adoption of SLA templates in order to reduce the problem of illiquid markets and improve the welfare of resource providers and users [44]. [45] urge the cloud providers to exploit cost and time trade-offs of users and manage resource allocation in a way that improved welfare of users as well as providers.

Strategy: Cloud resource markets under monopoly, competitive and oligopolistic market conditions were analysed and optimal strategy was identified [50]. Genetic algorithm based pricing and resource allocation strategy that identify the equilibrium price and determine virtual machine allocation were found to improve the consumer's utility and service provider's profits was discussed [47]. A Negotiation based mechanism was optimized to maximize a non-additive utility function comprising various goals namely revenue maximization, client classification, non-peak utilization and reputation [48].

Design: While most literature on cloud markets pertains to economic aspects of cloud markets, few works studied the design aspects of cloud markets. Cloud markets must be capable of handling trading requirements like use of several economic models, multiple user objectives, resource discovery and exchange requirements such as scalability, grid heterogeneity, security and fault tolerance [46]. Markets should be self-aware, have pre-defined goals, a monitoring component to track these goals, an analysis component to derive suitable action plans, a planning component to execute the actions and a knowledge component to store past histories. Metrics for self-aware markets include revenue, profits, transaction volume, costs, allocations, number of active traders, market liquidity etc. [49]. Table 3 provides a summary of key market oriented studies in literature.

4.2.2   Models

Research works across the four decision themes predominantly use simulation as a means to study the dynamics of their decision model. Simulations were used to study the effect of market based scheduling techniques [45], comparison and stress analysis of market models [46], effectiveness of market monitoring mechanisms [49], profitability in collaboration [41] and analysis of negotiation models [48]. Optimization was the next widely used methodology. In [23], the authors used an optimization approach to minimize costs in collaboration and maximize welfare in combinatorial auction based market mechanisms [42,43]. Other techniques or models include, application of Game theory to identify optimal strategies and Nash equilibrium in cloud markets [50], learning techniques in self-adapting SLA templates [44] and Genetic Algorithm in a market based resource allocation strategy [47].

4.2.3   Research Gaps

From Literature: While the need for cloud computing markets is fairly established and various market mechanisms illustrating the use of markets were proposed, the review highlights certain challenges as well. From a security and performance perspective, we need mystery shoppers, audits and a consortium to connect providers [39]. Communication and trading methodologies have to be developed for a multi-market environment [41,51]. Testing of market mechanisms have to be with real world data instead of synthetic data [23]. Market mechanisms should incorporate user behaviour and service quality expectations of the consumer [52]. From a decision modelling perspective, non-additive utility functions are yet to be developed.

Proposed by authors: The use of empirically validated functions in representing user preferences is scant. Most utility functions discussed found in the review are adhoc in nature and do not have support from behavioural research. One example is the application of decision functions from behavioural economic literature in electronic negotiations for procurement of cloud services [53].

5   Implications

This study explored in detail, several works dealing with decisions and models in cloud economics, with a focus on cloud pricing and markets. We believe that from a business perspective, this study enables a cloud consumer, vendor or a third party to readily identify parameters associated with a decision context, along with the models or techniques available to support the decision making. From a research perspective, we highlight several open questions discussed by the research community. The implications for researchers is that this study identifies opportunities where they can propose new decision contexts, new models, new parameters and improve existing methodologies. For example, through this review we found that, simulation was one of the preferred approaches in decision support. Similarly, price and cost were the parameters of choice in most of the studies reviewed. A researcher could improve a simulation approach or develop methodologies that consider parameters like reliability, trust, availability apart from cost or price.

Our study has contributed to existing body of research in cloud computing in the following ways. First, to the best of our knowledge, our study is the first systematic review and summary of decisions and models in economic aspects of cloud computing. Second,the depth of research focus and maturity on different business themes of cloud computing is presented. Third, we have collated the potential research opportunities via the research gaps section to guide researchers looking for nascent areas to work upon.

6   Summary and Limitations

In this review, we have attempted to provide a review of decisions and models in economic aspects of cloud computing. For the purpose of this article, we lay specific emphasis on two decision categories under cloud economics namely, pricing and markets. We can infer from the volume of articles (around 235) chosen from across various journals and conferences until 2012 that the general interest towards organizational implications of cloud is healthy. The fact that 67 research articles pertain to cloud economics indicates the level of importance and priority associated to this area by researchers. The top five research streams namely pricing, adoption, sourcing, resource allocation and markets account for nearly 55 % of the 157 articles reviewed. This presents an opportunity to explore and develop various models to support decision making in the less researched decision aspects like regulation, consumer behaviour, audits, contracting, agents and brokering, to name a few.

On limitations of the study, the search was restricted to nine databases and covered articles only till the year 2012. The search process did not cover books and technical reports. Further, 78 articles which were selected for the final review were inaccessible. The set of keywords used in the selection process might not exhaustively cover all decisions related to business aspects of cloud computing. The research framework in its current form does not allow classification of a paper under more than one category.

7   Conclusions and FutureWork

In this paper we provide a literature review on application of decision models to business aspects, more specifically economic aspects of cloud computing. We use a systematic research methodology to review literature and in this process reviewed 2891 abstracts and 157 completed articles. Based on the findings of our review, we propose a classification framework to organize decision making themes in cloud computing. Using this framework we review articles pertaining to the most widely researched themes under cloud economics namely pricing and markets. In general, while we find that though there were attempts to model consumer behaviour, such attempts have not been empirically supported, which in itself presents a research direction. Most studies focus on individual decision making, however the nature of cloud computing, demands for more studies involving group decision making. Studies should focus on integrating consumer behaviour with group decision making strategies.

We have provided an overview of the decisions and models applied to economic aspects of cloud computing and a framework to classify research themes. As part of future work, we would report our reviews on other widely researched areas namely adoption, resource allocation and sourcing decisions. This study has provided an empirical analysis on application of various models and techniques. We believe that study is useful to the research community in identifying potential research opportunities. From a practitioner's perspective, this research provides an overview of tools and models that apply to different decision making contexts and the parameters to consider in such contexts.

References

1. Flynn, M.: Some computer organizations and their effectiveness. IEEE Trans. Comput. **100**(9), 948–960 (1972)
2. Kitchenham, B.A., Charters, S.: Guidelines for performing systematic literature reviews in software engineering. EBSE Technical report, Software Engineering Group, Keele University (1972)
3. Buyya, R., Yeo, C., Venugopal, S., Broberg, J., Brandic, I.: Cloud computing and emerging IT platforms: vision, hype, and reality for delivering computing as the 5th utility. Future Gener. Comput. Syst. **25**(6), 599–616 (2009)
4. Forrester, Accessed 17 August 2012. http://www.cloudtweaks.com/2011/04/cloud-computing-market-will-top-241-billion-in-2020/ (2012)
5. Weinhardt, C., Anandasivam, A., Blau, B., Stosser, J.: Business models in the service world. IT Prof. **11**(2), 28–33 (2009)
6. Katzan Jr, H.: On an ontological view of cloud computing. J. Serv. Sci. **3**, 1 (2011)
7. Hofer, C.N., Karagiannis, G.: Cloud computing services: taxonomy and comparison. J. Internet Serv. Appl. **2**(2), 81–94 (2011)
8. Rimal, B., Choi, E., Lumb, I.: A taxonomy and survey of cloud computing systems. In: INC, IMS and IDC, NCM, Seoul, Korea (2009)
9. Dukaric, R., Juric, M.B.: Towards a unified taxonomy and architecture of cloud frameworks. Future Gener. Comput. Syst. **29**(5), 1196–1210 (2013)

10. Repschlaeger, J., Ruediger, Z., Wind S., Klaus, T.: A reference guide to cloud computing dimensions: infrastructure as a service classification framework. In: HICSS (2012)
11. Samimi, P., Patel, A.: Review of pricing models for grid and cloud computing. In: ISCI, KualaLampur, Malaysia (2011)
12. Kaisler, S., Money, W.H., Cohen, S.J.: A decision framework for cloud computing. In: HICSS (2012)
13. Marston, S., Li, Z., Bandyopadhyay, S., Zhang, J., Ghalsasi, A.: Cloud computing - the business perspective. Decis. Support Syst. **51**(1), 176–189 (2011)
14. Yang, H., Tate, M.: Where are we at with cloud computing? A descriptive literature review. In: ACIS (2009)
15. Zhang, Q., Cheng, L., Boutaba, R.: Cloud computing: state-of-the-art and research challenges. J. Internet Serv. Appl. **1**(1), 7–18 (2010)
16. Ho, W., Xu, X., Dey, P.: Multi-criteria decision making approaches for supplier evaluation and selection: a literature review. Eur. J. Oper. Res. **202**(1), 16–24 (2010)
17. Anandasivam, A., Premm, M.: Bid price control and dynamic pricing in clouds. In: ECIS, Verona, Italy (2009)
18. Andrzejak, A., Kondo, A., Yi, S.: Decision model for cloud computing under SLA constraints. In: MASCOTS, Miami, FL, pp. 257–266 (2010)
19. Ben-Yehuda, A., Ben-Yehuda, M., Schuster, A., Tsafrir, D.: Deconstructing Amazon EC2 spot instance pricing. In: CloudCom, Athens, Greece (2011)
20. Li, C.F.: Cloud computing system management under flat rate pricing. J. Netw. Syst. Manag. **19**(3), 305–318 (2011)
21. Daoud, A.A., Agarwal, S., Alpcan, T.: Brief announcement: cloud computing games: pricing services of large data centers. In: Keidar, I. (ed.) DISC 2009. LNCS, vol. 5805, pp. 309–310. Springer, Heidelberg (2009)
22. Hadji, M., Louati, W., Zeghlache, D.: Constrained pricing for cloud resource allocation. In: NCA, Cambridge (2011)
23. Hassan, M.M., Song, B., Huh, E.N.: A market-oriented dynamic collaborative cloud services platform. Ann. Telecommun. **65**(11–12), 669–688 (2010)
24. Li, H., Li, H.: A research of resource provider-oriented pricing mechanism based on game theory in cloud bank model. In: CSC, Hong Kong, China (2011)
25. Ibrahim, S., Bingsheng, H., Hai, J.: Towards pay-as-you-consume cloud computing. In: SCC, Washington, DC, USA (2011)
26. Javadi, B., Thulasiramy, R.K., Buyya, R.: Statistical modeling of spot instance prices in public cloud environments. In: UCC, Melbourne (2011)
27. Li, X., Lo, J.C.: Pricing and peak aware scheduling algorithm for cloud computing. In: ISGT, Piscataway, NJ, USA (2012)
28. Macias, M., Guitart, J.: A genetic model for pricing in cloud computing markets. In: ACM Symposium on Applied Computing, TaiChung, Taiwan (2011)
29. Mazzucco, M., Dumas, M.: Achieving performance and availability guarantees with spot instances. In: HPCC, Banff, AB, Canada (2011)
30. Mihailescu, M., Teo, Y.M.: Dynamic resource pricing on federated clouds. In: CCGrid, Melbourne (2010)
31. Roovers, J., Vanmechelen, K., Broeckhove, J.: A reverse auction market for cloud resources. In: Vanmechelen, K., Altmann, J., Rana, O.F. (eds.) GECON 2011. LNCS, vol. 7150, pp. 32–45. Springer, Heidelberg (2012)
32. Sharma, B., Thulasiram, R.K., Thulasiraman, P., Garg, S.K., Buyya, R.: Pricing cloud compute commodities: a novel financial economic model. In: CCGrid, Washington (2012)

33. Sowmya, K., Sundarraj, R.P.: Strategic bidding for cloud resources under dynamic pricing schemes. In: ISCOS, Surathkal, India (2012)
34. Teng, F., Magoules, F.: Resource pricing and equilibrium allocation policy in cloud computing. In: CIT, Bradford, UK (2010)
35. Wee, S.: Debunking real-time pricing in cloud computing. In: CCGrid, CA, USA (2011)
36. Woitaszek, M., Tufo, H.M.: Developing a cloud computing charging model for high-performance computing resources. In: CIT, Bradford, UK (2010)
37. Zaman, S., Grosu, D.: Combinatorial auction-based allocation of virtual machine instances in clouds. In: Cloudcom, Indianapolis, USA (2010)
38. Li, H., Liu, J., Tang, G.: A pricing algorithm for cloud computing resources. In: NCIS, Guilin, China (2011)
39. Laplante, P.: Econ 101 for cloud enthusiasts. IT Prof. **14**(1), 12–15 (2012)
40. Krieger, O., McGachey, P., Kanevsky, A.: Enabling a marketplace of clouds: VMware's vCloud director. Oper. Syst. Rev. **44**(4), 103–114 (2010)
41. Goiri, I., Guitart, J., Torres, J.: Characterizing cloud federation for enhancing providers' profit. In: IEEE 3rd International Conference on Cloud Computing, Miami, Florida, USA (2010)
42. Fujiwara, I., Aida, K., Ono, I.: Applying double-sided combinational auctions to resource allocation in cloud computing. In: SAINT, Seoul, Korea (2010)
43. Chen, Y.M., Yeh, H.M.: Autonomous adaptive agents for market-based resource allocation of cloud computing. In: ICMLC, Qingdao, China (2010)
44. Breskovic, I., Michael, M., Emeakaroha, V.C.: Achieving market liquidity through autonomic cloud market management. In: Brandic, I., Altmann, J. (eds.) Cloud Computing and Service Science, pp. 91–107. Springer, New York (2012)
45. Henzinger, T.A., Singh, A.V., Singh, V., Wies, T., Zufferey, D.: A marketplace for cloud resources. In: EMSOFT, New York (2010)
46. Garg, S.K., Vecchiola, C., Buyya, R.: Mandi: a market exchange for trading utility and cloud computing services. J. Supercomput. **64**(3), 1–22 (2011)
47. You, X., Xu, X., Wan, J., Yu, D.: RAS-M: resource allocation strategy based on market mechanism in cloud computing. In: ChinaGrid, Yantai, China (2009)
48. Macias, M., Guitart, J.: Using resource-level information into nonadditive negotiation models for cloud market environments. In: NOMS, Osaka, Japan (2010)
49. Breskovic, I., Hass, C., Caton, S., Brandic, I.: Towards self-awareness in cloud markets: a monitoring methodology. In: DASC, Sydney, Australia (2011)
50. Niyato, D., Chaisiri, S., Lee, B.S.: Economic analysis of resource market in cloud computing environment. In: APSCC, Jeju, South Korea (2009)
51. Garg, S.K., Versteeg, S., Buyya, R.: SMICloud: a framework for comparing and ranking cloud services. In: UCC, Melbourne, VIC, Australia (2011)
52. Zhang, Q., Zhu, Q., Boutaba, R.: Dynamic resource allocation for spot markets in cloud computing environments. In: UCC, Melbourne, VIC, Australia (2011)
53. Venkataraghavan, K., Sundarraj, R.P.: Incorporating intertemporal preferences in electronic negotiations for computing services: a mechanism and analysis. In: GDN Meeting, Stockholm, Sweden (2013)

Normative Requirements for Business Process Compliance

Mustafa Hashmi[1,2]([✉]), Guido Governatori[1,2], and Moe Thandar Wynn[1,2]

[1] NICTA, Queensland Research Laboratory, Brisbane, Australia
{mustafa.hashmi,guido.governatori}@nicta.com.au
[2] Queensland University of Technology (QUT), Brisbane, Australia
m.wynn@qut.edu.au

Abstract. Norms regulate the behaviour of their subjects and define what is legal and what is illegal. Norms typically describe the conditions under which they are applicable and the normative effects as a result of their applications. On the other hand, process models specify how a business operation or service is to be carried out to achieve a desired outcome. Norms can have a significant impact on how business operations are conducted and they can apply to the whole or a part of a business process. For example, they may impose conditions on the different aspects of a process (e.g., perform tasks in a specific sequence (control-flow), at a specific time or within a certain time frame (temporal aspect), by specific people (resources). We propose a framework that provides the formal semantics of the normative requirements for determining whether a business process complies with a normative document (where a normative document can be understood in a very broad sense, ranging from internal policies to best practice policies, to statutory acts). We also present a classification of normal requirements based on the notion of different types of obligations and the effects of violating these obligations.

Keywords: Norms · Regulatory compliance · Business process compliance

1 Introduction

Due to ever increasing pressure and demand from regulatory authorities, *compliance* has become a *must do activity* for every enterprise. Essentially, compliance corresponds to the enterprise's obedience to governing regulations enforced on its business operations. The demand for compliance can come from government regulations (e.g. the Sarbanes-Oxley Act, HIPPA, BASEL-III . . .), standards (ISO-9000, CoBIT . . .), and/or an enterprise's internal policies. Adherence with regulatory laws and internal controls essentially increase transparency and effective control over business operations.

NICTA is funded by the Australian Government through the Department of Communications and the Australian Research Council through the ICT Centre of Excellence Program.

J.G. Davis et al. (Eds.): ASSRI 2013, LNBIP 177, pp. 100–116, 2014.
DOI: 10.1007/978-3-319-07950-9_8, © Springer International Publishing Switzerland 2014

Service-Oriented Architecture (SOA) is one of the enablers for innovation in today's highly competitive business environment. Public and private enterprises alike are adopting new technologies to bring innovations into their business operations and to offer their core competencies as web services. Web services are often physically independent but logically interrelated pieces of services orchestrated to provide a specific functionality, and are designed by combining (possibly) disparate and often incongruous business processes from different enterprises [4]. In such a dynamic setting, the ability to trust that one another's internal processes that form the backbone of successful invocation of web services are compliant with regulations becomes even more crucial.

Business process models provide a high-level view on how business operations can be carried out to achieve a desired outcome. Business processes must behave within the defined limits of the regulatory guidelines (in legal context) called *norms*. Norms regulate business processes by imposing restrictions on *how business activities should be performed*. Any divergent behaviour may lead to termination of interactions or financial penalties [9]. Consider, a procurement process of a government agency which handles dynamic selection of vendors to place orders, which is implemented as a web service. Using such a web service, the agency can quickly place an order, receive and evaluate the quotes from suppliers. This process is subject to regulations, as such the procurement web service must be checked for compliance with relevant regulations before it can be deployed. A process model that reflects the behaviour of the procurement web service can be used to verify the effectiveness of regulations and policy controls.

The structure and properties of norms have been extensively studied by the field of Deontic Logic, Artificial Intelligence and Law, and Legal Reasoning (see, [15] for a comprehensive treatment with a formal and legal theory perspective). A number of researchers have incorporated the notion of process compliance in the service domain. Reference [13] deals with business rules driven business processes as service composition using various types of composition elements. The business rules considered in the framework are related to the structure of business processes. Reference [18] provides a formal characterisation of behavioural rules for business policy compliance for SOA which is again useful to check structural compliance of business processes. However, compliance is not only about how the activities should be performed (the control flow aspect) but also about what these activities do (data), and who performs the tasks (resources aspect).

Generally the compliance rules are written in a natural language (c.f. those that can be found in legal or policy documents). To enable automatic compliance checks of processes, these rules need to be formalised in a machine-readable format. Typically the formalisation of compliance rules is language dependent, and the choice of a formal language depends on the business analysts. In this paper, we carefully examine all different types of normative requirements which can be imposed upon the different perspectives of business processes and propose how these requirements can be captured in a formal manner without restricting ourselves to any particular formalism.

Hence, the aim of this paper is not to provide yet another framework for business process compliance; instead we provide conceptually sound foundations for the normative requirements for the normative component of the compliance problem. This is achieved by giving semantics of norms (obligations) in terms of the validity of a norm, effects of the violations; and the possible ways in which a business process can be executed.

In the next section, we provide a motivating scenario of a complaints handling process together with a set of normative requirements. The formal definitions of business process models are given in Sect. 3. Various types of normative requirements together with concrete examples for each type are discussed in Sect. 4. An illustration of how compliance checking can be carried out for the complaints handling process as well as an evaluation of a compliance framework, Regorous, based on the proposed set of normative requirements is provided in Sect. 5. Section 6 concludes the paper.

2   Motivating Scenario: A Complaints Handling Process

In this section, we provide a short description of the complaints handling process inspired by the LPMA[1] in New South Wales, Australia and required to follow a number of compliance requirements stated in an internal policy document.

Figure 1 depicts the overview of the procedure followed to resolve a complaint as a BPMN process model. The first step in the process is to determine whether a complaint is an oral complaint or a written complaint. If it is an

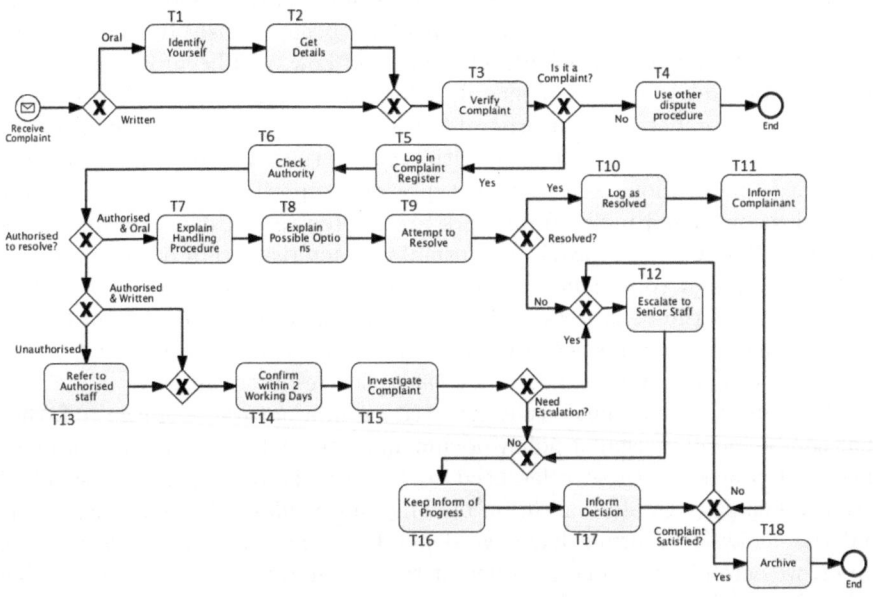

Fig. 1. Complaints handling process.

---

[1] The Land and Property Management Authority (LPMA), available at: http://www. lpma.nsw.gov.au/_data/assets/pdf_file/0004/25663/rth_Ch26_Aug_2009.pdf.

oral complaint, a staff member will identify himself and details are gathered from the complainant before proceeding. The staff member then verifies whether the received complaint meets the requirements of a legitimate complaint. If the received complaint does not meet the definition of a complaint, alternative dispute procedures are adopted (which is out of the scope of this process). After a complaint has been determined as a legitimate complaint, the staff member must decide whether (s)he has the appropriate authority to handle the complaint. If the staff is deemed to have the authority, then the complaint will go though the complaints handling process with the staff as its handler. Otherwise, the complaint is referred to an authorised staff and the complainant is informed. The authorised staff explains the process and the available options and attempts to resolve the complaint straight away if it is an oral complaint. If the complaint is resolved, then the complaint is logged as resolved and the complainant is informed about the decision.

For a written complaint, an authorised staff will confirm the complaint within two working days. A complaint is escalated to a senior staff if it cannot be resolved or the complainant is not satisfied or if the staff decides that it needs to be escalated. While the complaint is being investigated, the complainant is being kept informed. When a decision has been reached, the complainant is informed about the decision. When the complainant is satisfied with the decision, the complaint is closed off and archived.

Table 1 shows the policy excerpt of the compliant handling process.

Table 1. The compliance requirements of complaints handling process from LPMA, NSW.

Rule ID	Policy Description (Compliance Control/Specification)
R1	Staff receiving a complaint will aim to resolve it at the earliest opportunity.
R2	*Where the client is not satisfied with the initial response to the complaint, they will be given the option to progress the issue(s) through the formal complaints handling process outlined in department's complaints handling procedure.*
R3	*Staff will treat all complaints fairly and impartially, as is their obligation under the code of conduct.*
R4	*All complaints will be acknowledged within 2 working days of being initiated.*
R5	*All complainants kept informed about the progress of the matter, particularly if delays occur.*
R6	*Complainants will not be subject to any form of prejudice, loss of services, or be disadvantaged in any way as a result of having complained.*
R7	*Complaints will be treated with an appropriate level of confidentiality. Information about complaints will only be shared on a need–to–know basis, both within the agency and externally.*
R8	*Reasons will be provided for decisions made in relation to complaints received.*
R9	*If complaints do not meet the conditions in Section 9, the department may set limits or conditions on the handling of their complaints.*
R10	*Unauthorized staff cannot handle complaints (either oral or written).*

3   Formal Foundations of Business Process Compliance

Compliance is related to the behaviour of a process, where by the behaviour we understand how the process can be (*correctly*) executed. Thus we have to identify the traces of a process, where, from the compliance point of view a trace is the sequence of actions/tasks performed by the process. Compliance is not only about the tasks or actions undertaken but also what the tasks do, their artifacts and how they change the environment in which the process is situated. To capture this, we adopt the idea proposed in [14] and enrich processes with semantic annotations. These annotations are meant to capture the attributes, resources and other information related to the tasks in a process. We take an agnostic approach to the annotations themselves and assume that there is a suitable language to represent the annotations. We stipulate that the same language is used to represent both the annotations and the content of the normative requirements.

In this paper, we make use of *workflow-nets* (WF-Nets) [17], a subclass of Petri nets [12], to represent business processes. However, the definitions below can be easily modified for other representations of business processes.

Definition 1 (Petri Net). *A Petri Net is a tuple $PN = (P, T, F)$ where P is the set of places, T is the set of transitions, $P \cap T = \emptyset$ and $F \subseteq (P \times T) \cup (T \times P)$ is the flow relation.*

A Petri net is a collection of two types of nodes: *places* and *transitions*. Arcs connect one type of node to the other. For a node $x \in (P \cup T)$, $\bullet x$ denotes the set of inputs to x and $x\bullet$ denotes the set of outputs of x. The *state* of a Petri net is represented by a *marking* that describes the number of tokens in each place of a net.

A workflow net (WF-net) is defined as a subclass of Petri net with the following structural restrictions [16]. There is exactly one *source place* and exactly one *end place*. Every node in the graph is on a direct path from the source place to the end place.

Definition 2 (WF-net). *Given a Petri net $N = (P, T, F)$, the net N is a WF-net if and only if: (1) There is one source place $i \in P$ such that $\bullet i = \emptyset$. (2) There is one sink place $o \in P$ such that $o\bullet = \emptyset$. (3) Every node $x \in P \cup T$ is on a path from i to o.*

Definition 3 (Enabling and Firing Rules of a WF-net). *Given a WF-net $N = (P, T, F)$, a transition $t \in T$ and a marking M of N, t is enabled at M, denoted as $M[t\rangle$, if and only if, there is at least one token each in all $p \in \bullet t$. If $M[t\rangle$ holds and transition t is fired, a new marking M' of N is reached, which removes a token each from each $p \in \bullet t$ and puts a token in each $p \in t\bullet$. This is denoted as $M \xrightarrow{t} M'$.*

Definition 4 (Occurrence sequence). *Given a WF-net $N = (P, T, F)$ and markings $M, M_1, \ldots, M_n$ of N, if $M \xrightarrow{t_1} M_1 \xrightarrow{t_2} \cdots \xrightarrow{t_n} M_n$ holds then $\sigma = \langle t_1, t_2, \ldots, t_n \rangle$ is an occurrence sequence leading from M to M_n.*

The initial marking of a WF-net is i, where there is one token in the source place i, and the end marking of a WF-net is o. A *trace* in a WF-net represents an occurrence sequence from the initial marking i to the end marking o.

Definition 5 (Labeled WF-Net). *A labeled WF-net $N = (P, T, F, l)$ is a WF-net (P, T, F) with a labeling function $l \in T \twoheadrightarrow \mathcal{U}_A$, where $\mathcal{U}_A$ is some universe of activity labels. Let $\sigma_v = \langle a_1, a_2, \ldots, a_n \rangle \in \mathcal{U}_A{}^*$ be a sequence of activities and M, M' be two markings of N. $M[\sigma_v \triangleright M'$ if and only if there is a sequence $\sigma \in T^*$ such that $M[\sigma\rangle M'$ and $l(\sigma) = \sigma_v$.*

With this definition we only have the *visible and labeled* transitions in the net. For a set of traces of a workflow net $\mathfrak{T}^+(N)$, $\mathfrak{T}^+ = \{\sigma_\Theta | i[\sigma_\Theta\rangle o\}$ is the set of all visible traces in the net, where $\Theta = \{\sigma_1, \sigma_2, \ldots, \sigma_n\}$ is a set of all occurrence sequences. The idea behind the notion of a labelled WF-Net is that a trace of visible transitions corresponds to a possible execution sequence of the process, where the visible transitions correspond to the tasks executed by the process.

Next, we look at how a WF-net can be annotated with compliance requirements. We begin with the definition of the language.

Definition 6 (Literal). *Let A be the set of all atomic propositions. The set of literals is $\mathfrak{L} = \{a, \neg a | a \in A\}$.*

A consistent set of literals can be understood as either a (partial) interpretation (i.e., an assignment of truth value) or equivalently a (partial) description of a state.

Definition 7 (Consistent Set). *A set of literals L is consistent if and only if L does not contain any pair of literals $l, \neg l$.*

Definition 8 (Annotation). *Let N be a WF-net and $\mathfrak{T}^+$ be the set of visible traces of N. An annotation ann is a function $Ann : \mathfrak{T}^+ \times \mathbb{N} \mapsto 2^\mathfrak{L}$ such that for every $t \in \mathfrak{T}^+$ and every $n \in \mathbb{N}$, $Ann(t, n)$ is a consistent set of literals.*

Annotations enable a process to have states attached to the tasks. The function $Ann(t, n)$ returns the state obtained after the execution of the n-th task (visible transition) in the (visible) trace t.

Definition 9 (Annotated WF-Net). *An annotated WF-net is a pair $\langle N, Ann \rangle$, where $N = (P, T, F, l)$ is a labeled WF-net, and Ann is an annotation.*

In an annotated WF-net, each visible trace uniquely determines the sequence of states obtained by executing that trace. Thus, in what follows whenever clear from the context we use trace to refer to a sequence of tasks, and the corresponding sequence of states.

Remark 1. It is not within the scope of this paper to describe how the sequences of states corresponding of the execution of a process are obtained. The task of specifying how the function *Ann* is implemented is left to specific compliance applications.

4   Normative Requirements

Norms regulate the behaviour of their subjects and define what is legal and what is illegal. Norms typically describe the conditions under which they are applicable and the normative effects they produce when applied. Reference [5] provides a comprehensive list of normative effects. From the compliance perspective the normative effects of importance are the deontic effects. The basic deontic effects –from which others deontic effects can be derived, see [15]– are: *obligation, prohibition* and *permission.*

Let us start by consider the basic definitions for such concepts:[2]

Obligation A situation, an act, or a course of action to which a bearer is legally
   bound, and if it is not achieved or performed results in a violation.
Prohibition A situation, an act, or a course of action which a bearer should
   avoid, and if it is achieved results in a violation.
Permission Something is permitted if the obligation or prohibition to the contrary does not hold.

Obligations and prohibitions are constraints that limit the behaviour of processes. The different between obligations and prohibitions and other types of constraints is that they can be violated. On the other hand, *permissions* are constraints that cannot be violated and thus, permissions do not play a direct role in compliance. Instead, they can be used to determine that there are no obligations or prohibitions to the contrary, or to derive other deontic effects. Legal reasoning and legal theory typically assume a strong relationship between obligations and prohibitions: the prohibition of A is the obligation of $\neg A$ (the opposite of A), and then if A is obligatory, then $\neg A$ is forbidden [15]. In this paper we will subscribe to this position, given that our focus here is not on how to determine what is prescribed by a set of norms and how to derive it. Accordingly, we can restrict our analysis to the notion of an *obligation.*

Compliance means to identify whether a process violates a set of obligations. Thus, the first step is to determine *whether* and *when* an obligation is in force. Hence, an important aspect of the study of obligations is to understand the lifespan of an obligation and its implications on the activities carried out in a process. As norms give the conditions of applicability of obligations, the next question is *how long does an obligation hold for.* Essentially, a norm can specify that an obligation is in force at a particular time point only, or more often, a norm indicates when an obligation comes in force. An obligation is considered

---

[2] Here we consider the definition of such concepts given by the OASIS LegalRuleML
   working group. http://www.oasis-open.org/apps/org/workgroup/legalruleml/.

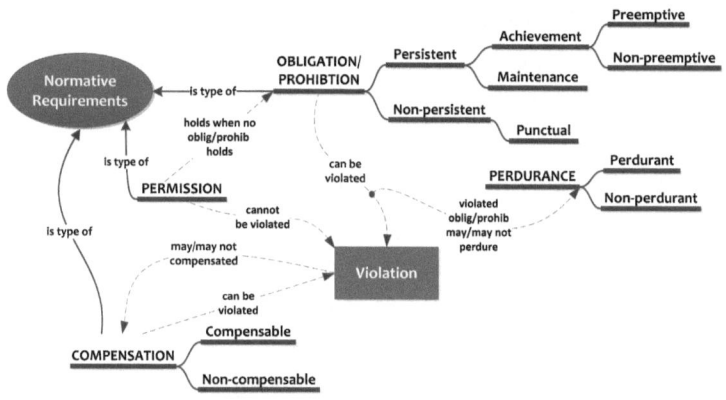

Fig. 2. Normative requirements: classes and relationship

to remain in force until it is terminated or removed. In the first case we speak of *non-persistent obligations* and *persistent obligations* in the second.

A *persistent obligation* that needs to be obeyed for all time instances within the interval in which it is in force is a *maintenance obligation*. If achieving the content of the obligation at least once is enough to fulfill it, then it is considered an *achievement obligation*. For an *achievement obligation*, another aspect to consider is whether the obligation could be fulfilled even before the obligation is actually in force. If this is allowed, then we have a *preemptive obligation*, otherwise the obligation is a *non-preemptive obligation*. In contrast, a *non-persistent obligation* needs to be obeyed for the instance it is in force, and categorised as a *punctual obligation*. For *punctual obligations* the obligation contents are immediately achieved otherwise a violation is triggered.

An obligation of any type can be violated. A *violation* does not always imply the consequent termination of or impossibility to continue a business process. Certain violations can be compensated for, and processes with compensated violations are still compliant [7,10]. For example, contracts typically contain compensatory clauses specifying penalties and other sanctions triggered by breaches of contract clauses [6]. However, not all violations are compensable, and uncompensated violations mean that a process is not compliant. The effects of a violation on the obligation that has been violated also need to be considered. If the obligation persists after being violated, it is a *perdurant obligation*, if it does not, then we have a *non-perdurant obligation*.

Figure 2 illustrates possibilities and relationships for the deontic effects we discussed in this section. The classification provided has been obtained in a systematic and exhaustive way when one considers the aspect of validity of obligations (or prohibitions), and the effects of violations on them, namely: whether a violation can be compensated for, and whether an obligation persists after being violated.

4.1   Modeling Obligations

In this section we provide the formal definitions underpinning the notion of compliance. In particular we formally define the different types of obligations depicted in Fig. 2.

Definition 10 (Obligation in force). *Given a WF-net N, let $\mathfrak{T}^+$ be the set of visible traces of N. We define a function Force* $: \mathfrak{T}^+ \times \mathbb{N} \mapsto 2^{\mathfrak{L}}$.

The function *Force* associates to each task in a trace a set of literals, where these literals represent the obligations in force for that combination of task and trace. These are among the obligations that the process has to fulfill to comply with a given normative framework. Next, we define how and when the process has to fulfill the various obligations (depending on their type) to be deemed compliant.

Remark 2. As in Remark 1 we abstract from mechanisms to establish which obligations are in force and when. This is left for specific compliance implementations.

Definition 11 (Punctual Obligation). *Given a WF-net N and a visible trace $t \in \mathfrak{T}^+(N)$, an obligation o is a* punctual obligation *in t if and only if*

$$\exists n \in \mathbb{N} : o \notin Force(t, n-1),\ o \notin Force(t, n+1),\ o \in Force(t, n).$$

A punctual obligation o is violated in t if and only if $o \notin Ann(t, n)$.

A punctual obligation is an obligation in force in one task of a trace. The obligation is violated if what the obligation prescribes is not achieved in or done by the task, meaning that the literal not being in the set of literals associated to the task in the trace.

Definition 12 (Achievement Obligation). *Given a WF-net N and a visible trace $t \in \mathfrak{T}^+(N)$, an obligation o is an* achievement obligation *in t if and only if*

$$\exists n < m \in \mathbb{N} : o \notin Force(t, n-1),\ o \notin Force(t, m+1), \forall k : n \leq k \leq m, o \in Force(t, k)$$

An achievement obligation o is violated in t if and only if

- *o is preemptive and $\forall k : k \leq m,\ o \notin Ann(t, k)$;*
- *o is non-preemptive and $\forall k : n \leq k \leq m,\ o \notin Ann(t, k)$.*

An achievement obligation is in force in a contiguous set of tasks in a trace. The violation depends on whether we have a preemptive or a non-preemptive obligation. For a preemptive obligation *o* we have a violation if no state before the last task in which *o* is in force has *o* in its annotations; while for a non-preemptive obligation the set of states is restricted to those defined by the interval in which the obligation is in force.

Example 1. Australian Telecommunications Consumers Protection Code 2012 (TCPC 2012). Article 8.2.1.

A Supplier must take the following actions to enable this outcome:

(a) **Demonstrate fairness, courtesy, objectivity and efficiency:** Suppliers must demonstrate, fairness and courtesy, objectivity, and efficiency by:
  (i) Acknowledging a Complaint:
      A. immediately where the Complaint is made in person or by telephone;
      B. within 2 Working Days of receipt where the Complaint is made by: email; . . . .

The obligation to acknowledge a compliant made in person or by phone (8.2.1.a.i.A) is a punctual obligation, since it has to be done 'immediately' while receiving it. 8.2.1.a.i.B on the other hand is an achievement obligation since the clause specifies a deadline to achieve it. It is also a non-preemptive obligation as it is not possible to acknowledge a complaint before receipt. Clause (3) in Example 2 illustrates a preemptive obligation.

Example 2. Australian National Consumer Credit Protection Act 2009. Schedule 1, Part 2, Section 20: Copy of contract for debtor.

(1) If a contract document is to be signed by the debtor and returned to the credit provider, the credit provider must give the debtor a copy to keep.
(2) A credit provider must, not later than 14 days after a credit contract is made, give a copy of the contract in the form in which it was made to the debtor.
(3) Subsection (2) does not apply if the credit provider has previously given the debtor a copy of the contract document to keep.

Definition 13 (Maintenance Obligation). *Given a WF-Net N and a visible trace $t \in \mathfrak{T}^+(N)$, an obligation o is a* maintenance obligation *in t if and only if*

$$\exists n < m \in \mathbb{N} : o \notin Force(t, n-1), \ o \notin Force(t, m+1), \forall k : n \leq k \leq m, o \in Force(t, k)$$

A maintenance obligation o is violated in t if and only if

$$\exists k : n \leq k \leq m, o \notin Ann(t, k).$$

Similarly to an achievement obligation, a maintenance obligation is in force in an interval. The difference is that the obligation has to be complied with for all tasks in the interval, otherwise a violation is triggered.

Example 3. TCPC 2012. Article 8.2.1.

A supplier must take the following actions to enable this outcome:

(v) not taking Credit Management action in relation to a specified disputed amount that is the subject of an unresolved Complaint in circumstances where the Supplier is aware that the Complaint has not been resolved to the satisfaction of the Consumer and is being investigated by the Supplier, the TIO or a relevant recognised third party;

In this example, as it is often the case, a maintenance obligation implements a prohibition. Specifically, the prohibition to initiate a particular type of activity until either a particular event takes place or a state is reached.

The next three definitions (Definitions 14, 15, Definition 16) capture the notion of compensation of a violation. A compensation is a set of penalties or sanctions imposed on the violator, and fulfilling them makes amends for the violation. The first step is to define what a compensation is. A compensation is a set of obligations in force after a violation of an obligation. Since the compensations are obligations themselves they can be violated, and they can be compensable as well, thus we need a recursive definition for the notion of compensated obligation.

Definition 14 (Compensation). *A compensation is a function Comp :* $\mathfrak{L} \mapsto 2^{\mathfrak{L}}$.

Definition 15 (Compensable Obligation). *Given a WF-Net N and a visible trace* $t \in \mathfrak{T}^+(N)$, *an obligation o is* compensable *in T if and only if Comp(o)* $\neq \emptyset$ *and* $\forall o' \in Comp(o), \exists n \in \mathbb{N} : o' \in Force(t, n)$.

Definition 16 (Compensated Obligation). *Given a WF-Net N and a visible trace* $t \in \mathfrak{T}^+(N)$, *an obligation o is* compensated *in t if and only if it is violated and for every* $o' \in Comp(o)$ *either: (1) o' is not violated in t, or (2) o' is compensated in t.*

For a stricter notion, i.e., a compensated compensation does not amend the violation the compensation was meant to compensate, we can simply remove the recursive call, thus removing 2. from the above condition.

Compensations can be used for two purposes. The first is to specify alternative, less ideal outcomes. The second is to capture sanctions and penalties. Examples 4 and 5 below illustrate, respectively, these two usages.

Example 4. TCPC 2012. Article 8.1.1.
A Supplier must take the following actions to enable this outcome:

(a) **Implement a process**: implement, operate and comply with a Complaint handling process that: (vii) requires all complaints to be:
   A. Resolved in an objective, efficient and fair manner; and
   B. escalated and managed under the Supplier's internal escalation process if requested by the Consumer or a former Customer.

Example 5. YAWL Deed of Assignment, Clause 5.2.[3]
Each Contributor indemnifies and will defend the Foundations against any claim, liability, loss, damages, cost and expenses suffered or incurred by the Foundations as a result of any breach of the warranties given by the Contributor under **clause 5.1**.

---

[3] http://www.yawlfoundation.org/files/YAWLDeedOfAssignmentTemplate.pdf, retrieved on March 28, 2013.

The final definition is that of a perdurant obligation. The intuition behind it is that there is a deadline by when the obligation has to be fulfilled. If it is not fulfilled by the deadline then a violation is raised, but the obligation is still in force. Typically, the violation of a perdurant obligation triggers a penalty. If an perdurant obligation is not fulfilled in time, then the process has to account for the original obligation as well as the penalties associated with the violation.

Definition 17 (Perdurant Obligation). *Given a WF-net N and a visible trace $t \in \mathfrak{T}^+(N)$, an obligation o is a* perdurant obligation *in t if and only if*

$$\exists n < m \in \mathbb{N} : o \notin Force(t, n-1),\ o \notin Force(t, m+1), \forall k : n \leq k \leq m, o \in Force(t, k)$$

A perdurant obligation o is violated in t if and only if

$$\exists k : n < k < m,\ \forall j \leq k, o \notin Ann(t, j)$$

Consider again Example 1. Clauses TCPC 8.2.1.a.i.A and 8.2.1.a.i.B state the deadlines to acknowledge a complaint, but 8.2.1.a.i prescribes that complaints have to be acknowledged. Thus, if a complaint is not acknowledged within the prescribed time then either clause A or B are violated, but the supplier still has the obligation to acknowledge the complaint. Thus the obligation in clause (i) is a perdurant obligation.

4.2 Business Process Compliance

The set of (visible) traces of a given business process describes the behaviour of the process insofar as it provides a description of all possible ways in which the process can be correctly executed. Accordingly, for the purpose of defining what it means for a process to be compliant, we will consider a process as the set of its (visible) traces. Intuitively a process is compliant with a given set of norms if it does not violate the norms. As it is possible to perform a business process in many different ways, we can have two notions of compliance, namely:

A process is (fully) compliant with a normative system if it is impossible to violate the norms while executing the process.

A process is (partially) compliant with a normative system if it is possible to execute the process without violating the norms.

We have a fully compliant process if no matter in which way the process is executed, its execution does not violates the normative system. A partially compliant process is one where there is an execution of the process that does not violate the norms. Based on this intuition, we provide the definitions for trace compliance and process compliance.

Definition 18 (Compliant Trace). *Given a WF-net N and a trace t in $\mathfrak{T}^+$. Let $O(t)$ be the set of obligations in force in t, i.e., $O(t) = \bigcup_{n \in \mathbb{N}} Force(t, n)$.*

1. *A trace t is* strongly compliant *if and only if no obligation $o \in O(t)$ is violated in t.*
2. *A trace t is* weakly compliant *if and only if every violated obligation $o \in O(t)$ is compensated in t.*

Definition 19 (Compliant Process). *Let N be a WF-net.*

1. *N is* fully compliant *if and only if every trace $t \in \mathfrak{T}^+(N)$ is compliant.*
2. *N is* partially compliant *if and only if there exists a compliant trace $t \in \mathfrak{T}^+(N)$.*

Notice that a possible refinement of Definition 19 is possible to distinguish between strongly and weakly compliant processes. This is achieved by passing the strongly/weakly parameter to the traces. For example a process is strongly compliant if all its visible traces are strongly compliant.

The definitions given in this section (apart from the Definition 19) can be used across the entire life-cycle of a process: design-time, run-time and post-execution analysis. As we pointed out in Remarks 1 and 2 the states and obligations in force have to be determined by specific compliance checking implementations. For example, the annotations associated to a task at run-time or log-analysis will be obtained from the running instance or extracted from the log and the data sources related to the process, while at design-time such information can be provided by business analysts or obtained from the schemas of the databases and data sources linked to the process. Definition 19 can be used at design time in what is called compliance-by-design [10,14], i.e., verifying before deploying a process that the process complies with given regulations. Clearly, the definition is not suitable for checking compliance at run-time (also called conformance) or auditing (log analysis), since it is possible that some of the possible visible traces are never executed (run-time) or were not executed (auditing). For these two cases, one has to use Definition 18 instead applied to the executed traces, and to the traces of instances of a process recorded in a log.

5   Compliance Checking of the Complaints Handling Process

We now provide a concrete example of compliance checking based on the complaints handling process shown earlier. Table 2 describes the applicable compliance rules and their types. These rules are relevant to one or more tasks in the complaints handling process. For example, *Rule4* is relevant to Task T_{14}, suggesting that all received complaints must be acknowledged within 2 working days when received. Similarly, *Rule9* intends to verify the legitimacy of complaints which relates to Task T_3 in the process. Consider the following trace t.

$$t : \langle T_3, T_5, T_6, T_7, T_8, T_9, T_{10}, T_{11}, T_{18} \rangle$$

The obligation expressed by $R1$ is in force from Task T_5, and it will be associated with any following task until the obligation has been fulfilled. Whether $R2$ is

Table 2. The ruleID and types of norms from the complaints handling process.

Rule ID	Rule Type
R1	Obligation, Achievement, Non-preemptive, Non-perdurant
R2	Obligation, Achievement, Preemptive, Perdurant
R3	Obligation, Maintenance, Perdurant
R4	Obligation, Achievement, Non-preemptive, Perdurant
R5	Obligation, Achievement, Non-preemptive, Non-perdurant
R6	Obligation, Maintenance, Perdurant
R7	Obligation, Maintenance, Perdurant
R8	Obligation, Achievement, Non-preemptive, Perdurant
R9	Permission
R10	Prohibition, Maintenance, Perdurant

relevant or not for a trace depends on the decision node after T_9, and it is not triggered in the trace given. Whereas $R3$ is in force from the beginning to the end of the process, and it is in all traces.

Evaluation

To conclude this section we report on an evaluation of the framework using Regorous. Regorous is an implementation of the compliance checking methodology proposed by Governatori and Sadiq [10, 14] where the normative provisions relevant to a process are encoded in PCL [8,9] and the tasks of a process are annotated with sets of literals taken from the language used to model the norms. The Regorous module to check compliance generates the traces of the given process and cumulates the annotations attached to tasks using an update semantics to determine the state corresponding to a task in a trace (i.e., in case a literal from the then current task is the complementary of from a previous task, we remove the old literal and we insert the new one). PCL offers support for all types of obligations described in the previous section, and for every step in a trace, it retrieves the state corresponding to the task being examined. Based on state PCL determines the obligations in force for the current task. Finally, it checks if the obligations have been fulfilled or violated based on the semantics discussed in the previous section. For the full details of PCL mechanisms, see [9].

Regorous was tested against the Australian Telecommunication Consumers Protection Code (TCPC) 2012. The code specifically mandates that every Australian entity operating in the telecommunication sector has to provide a certification that their day to day operations complies with the code.

The test was limited to TCPC Section 8 concerning the management and handling of consumer complaints. The section was manually mapped to PCL. The section of the code contains approximately 100 commas, in addition to approximately 120 terms given in the Definitions and Interpretation section of the code. The mapping resulted in 176 PCL rules, containing 223 PCL (atomic) propositions (literals). The formalisation of TCPC Section 8 required all types of obligations described in Sect. 4. Table 3 reports the number of distinct occurrences and, in parenthesis, the total number of instances (some effects can have different conditions under which they are effective).

Table 3. Number and types of obligations and permissions in Section 8 of TCPC

Punctual Obligation	5	(5)
Achievement Obligation	90	(110)
Preemptive	41	(46)
Non preemptive	49	(64)
Non perdurant	5	(7)
Maintenance Obligation	11	(13)
Prohibition	7	(9)
Non perdurant	1	(4)
Permission	9	(16)
Compensation	2	(2)

The evaluation was carried out in cooperation with an industry partner operating in the sector of the code. The PCL formalisation of TCPC Secti on 8 was reviewed and informally approved for the purpose of the exercise by the regulator. The industry partner did not have formalised business processes. Thus, we worked with domain experts from the industry partner (who had not been previously exposed to BPM technology, but who were familiar with the industry code) to draw process models to capture the existing complaints handling and management procedures and other related activities covered by TCPC Section 8. As result we generated and annotated six process models. Five out of the six models are limited in size and they can be checked for compliance in seconds. We were able to identify non-compliance issues in the processes and to rectify them. In the simplest and most frequent cases the modifications required were just to ensure that some type of information was recorded in the databases associated to the processes. Other cases needed the addition of simple tasks either after or before other tasks (e.g., make customer aware of documents detailing the escalation procedure after an unsatisfactory outcome of a non-escalated complaint). The above two types of non-compliance were detected by unfulfilled achievement obligations and they were the results of new requirements in the 2012 version of the code. Another case of non-compliance was related to ensuring that a particular activity does not happen in a part of the process. Finally, there were some cases where combination of the above issues were needed (a novel way to handle in person or by phone complaints) where totally new sub-processes were designed.

The largest process contains 41 tasks, 12 decision points, xor splits, (11 binary, 1 ternary). The shortest path in the model has 6 tasks, while the longest path consists of 33 tasks (with 2 loops), and the longest path without loop is 22 tasks long. The time taken to verify compliance for this process amounts approximately to 40 s on MacBook Pro 2.2 GHz Intel Core i7 processor with 8 GB of RAM (limited to 4 GB in Eclipse).

6   Conclusions

In the SOA and cloud computing domains, a number of approaches have offered several classifications of business rules for compliance checking. Reference [1] classifies compliance rules from various regulatory frameworks for cloud-based compliant workflows. Spanning over nine categories their classification comprises three main rules classes relevant to either the control-flow or the data flow of workflow models. These rules classes are then formalised into Petri nets for automated detection of non-compliant behaviour. Reference [3] provides a taxonomy of high level pattern-based compliance constraints for business processes. The compliance patterns are divided into three distinct classes of patterns; namely *atomic, composite, and timed*. These patterns are then formalised using temporal logic for generating the formal expressions for checking the compliance of business processes before actual deployment. Primarily the classification of normative requirements provided in these frameworks is useful for structural compliance checking only. In addition, these studies do not address *how to model* and *reason about* the normative component of compliance.

Contrary to that, we have provided its formal semantics in terms of what constitutes a violation, and this analysis was done based on the idea of (possible) executions of a process. In addition, for each type of normative requirement we have provided concrete examples from clauses of statutory/legislative acts corresponding to the requirement. With formalised compliance rules, we can specify the different types of rules describing various deontic modalities e.g. obligations, permissions etc. As result, business processes can be annotated with rules for compliance checking purposes. This means that any system (either SOA based or other) for checking whether real life business processes are compliant with real life regulations have to handle such all normative requirements.

One possible use of the framework is to compare different systems, logics, and frameworks for business process compliance. We plan to carry out such investigations. A second use is to study the (formal) properties of the problem of checking whether a business process is compliant. A first step in this direction is [2] proving that whether a structured business process (without loops) complies with a set of achievement obligations is already an NP-complete problem. Compliance is conceived as a type of soundness property of process, and thus the result must be compared to checking the soundness of process, and for the same class of processes (e.g., structured without loops) this can be done in linear time (see, e.g., [11]). This opens another area where the framework can be applied, namely to identify computationally tractable subclasses of the business process compliance problem.

References

1. Accorsi, R., Lowis, L., Sato, Y.: Automated certification for compliant cloud-based business processes. Bus. Inf. Syst. Eng. **3**(3), 145–154 (2011)
2. Tosatto, S.C., Governatori, G., Kelsen, P., van der Torre, L.: Business process compliance is hard. Technical report, NICTA (2012)

3. Elgammal, A., Turetken, O., van den Heuvel, W.-J., Papazoglou, M.: Root-cause analysis of design-time compliance violations on the basis of property patterns. In: Maglio, P.P., Weske, M., Yang, J., Fantinato, M. (eds.) ICSOC 2010. LNCS, vol. 6470, pp. 17–31. Springer, Heidelberg (2010)

4. Elgammal, A., Turetken, O., van den Heuvel, W.-J., Papazoglou, M.: On the formal specification of regulatory compliance: a comparative analysis. In: Maximilien, E.M., Rossi, G., Yuan, S.-T., Ludwig, H., Fantinato, M. (eds.) ICSOC 2010. LNCS, vol. 6568, pp. 27–38. Springer, Heidelberg (2011)

5. Gordon, T.F., Governatori, G., Rotolo, A.: Rules and norms: requirements for rule interchange languages in the legal domain. In: Governatori, G., Hall, J., Paschke, A. (eds.) RuleML 2009. LNCS, vol. 5858, pp. 282–296. Springer, Heidelberg (2009)

6. Governatori, G.: Representing business contracts in RuleML. Int. J. Coop. Inf. Syst. **14**(2–3), 181–216 (2005)

7. Governatori, G., Milosevic, Z.: Dealing with contract violations: formalism and domain specific language. In: EDOC 2005, pp. 46–57 (2005)

8. Governatori, G., Rotolo, A.: A conceptually rich model of business process compliance. In: Proceeding of APCCM'10, vol. 110, pp. 3–12 (2010)

9. Governatori, G., Rotolo, A.: Norm compliance in business process modeling. In: Dean, M., Hall, J., Rotolo, A., Tabet, S. (eds.) RuleML 2010. LNCS, vol. 6403, pp. 194–209. Springer, Heidelberg (2010)

10. Governatori, G., Sadiq, S.: The journey to business process compliance. In: Cardoso, J., van der Aalst, W. (eds.) Handbook of Research on Business Process Management, pp. 426–454. IGI Global, Hershey (2009)

11. Kiepuszewski, B., ter Hofstede, A.H.M., Bussler, C.J.: On structured workflow modelling. In: Wangler, B., Bergman, L.D. (eds.) CAiSE 2000. LNCS, vol. 1789, pp. 431–445. Springer, Heidelberg (2000)

12. Murata, T.: Petri nets: properties, analysis and applications. Proc. IEEE **77**(4), 541–580 (1989)

13. Orriëns, B., Yang, J., Papazoglou, M.P.: A framework for business rule driven service composition. In: Benatallah, B., Shan, M.-C. (eds.) TES 2003. LNCS, vol. 2819, pp. 14–27. Springer, Heidelberg (2003)

14. Sadiq, W., Governatori, G., Namiri, K.: Modeling control objectives for business process compliance. In: Alonso, G., Dadam, P., Rosemann, M. (eds.) BPM 2007. LNCS, vol. 4714, pp. 149–164. Springer, Heidelberg (2007)

15. Sartor, G.: Legal Reasoning: A Cognitive Approach to the Law. Springer, Dordrecht (2005)

16. van der Aalst, W.M.P.: The application of petri nets to workflow management. J. Circuits Syst. Comput. **8**(1), 21–66 (1998)

17. van der Aalst, W.M.P.: Workflow verification: finding control-flow errors using petri-net-based techniques. In: van der Aalst, W.M.P., Desel, J., Oberweis, A. (eds.) Business Process Management. LNCS, vol. 1806, p. 161. Springer, Heidelberg (2000)

18. Weigand, H., van den Heuvel, W.-J., Hiel, M.: Business policy compliance in service-oriented systems. Inf. Syst. **36**(4), 791–807 (2011)

Author Index